AF552319

THE BOOK

This simple and practical book is a guide to the Fey Tarot.
Designed both for beginner and experienced alike, it shows how to use
the cards and also how to look at them with the eyes of the soul.
At the same time, it opens up the many different
nuances of the deck so it can be used to its maximum potential.

THE TAROT

These tarot cards have an unusual strength.
They communicate directly with the soul and are
a deep well that is never emptied.
Easy to understand, they offer subtle insights and
gentle suggestions and, like all things magic, they avoid the ordinary.
Transporting the spirit of whoever uses them into a Fey world,
one is then led lightly home, wiser and enriched.

The Tarot can be considered a lucid and clear mirror which at times presents not only the reflected image but also allows unexpressed possibilities and the infinite potential of our universe to be realized through them. This is the Magic of the Tarot: a window of possibilities, and insight into the future...

ABOUT THE AUTHORS

Mara Aghem, an extraordinary painter, is a deeply joyful and cheerful person, feelings which are expressed through her paintings. She is considered one of the most promising Italian painters of the next generation.
For more info: *http://www.mara-aghem.com*

Riccardo Minetti, consultant and editor for Edizioni d'Arte Lo Scarabeo since 1996. In the past few years he has collaborated in the creation of certain decks, including the Etruscan Tarot.

the Fey tarot

Dreams, Joy and Magic

written by Riccardo Minetti and illustrated by Mara Aghem

LO SCARABEO

Fey Tarot

First English Edition
First printing, 2002

Italian Title: Tarocchi delle Fate

By Riccardo Minetti
Cover image and illustrations by Mara Aghem
Translation by Elizabeth O'Neill and Harriet Graham

Editing and book design:
Pietro Alligo, Riccardo Minetti, Harriet Graham

Printed in the EU
A4 servizi grafici s.n.c.
Via F.lli Meliga 3A - 10034 Chivasso - Torino - Italy

Lo Scarabeo S.r.l.
Via Varese 15c 10152 - Torino - Italy
info@loscarabeo.com - www.loscarabeo.com

ISBN 88-8395257-X

Table of Contents

HOW TO USE THIS BOOK

This book is a manual for the Fey Tarot, and much more.

Written in an informal manner it is also a recollection of how this deck came to be created, in part to make the book more readable and enjoyable, but most of all to involve the reader in the creative process. By following this creative act, the reader will not only have a greater understanding of the Fey Tarot but also of Tarots in general.

In fact, through understanding the link between image and meaning, it is possible to start gaining a visual, universal method of interpretation, valid for any deck of Tarot.

In the book, space is also given to the Fey vision and various 'fey' myths in the world, not just from Anglo-Saxon folklore, in an attempt to highlight those universal characteristics of magic and nature that many cultures have in common.

Prior to the completion of each Arcana, it was necessary to create and design several sketches and studies.
These black and white drawings, while lacking the evocative power of the final Arcana, may nevertheless be interesting to the mind's eye.

By looking attentively at the drawings, it is possible to gain an insight into how the Tarot card has been created, glimpsing the previous version of the card. Different faces, postures and expressions seem to tell the story of the symbols of the card and how they developed on their own and slowly took their rightful place.
Looking at these sketches may sometimes seem like a window to an alternative world, to a different Arcana. When I look at the images, I see all the hard work and the joy behind the realisation of this deck, and they never fail to move me.

INTRODUCTION

The word "fey" comes from Anglo-Saxon folklore, which in turn came from Germanic and Saxon lore.

Fey, fairies, pixies, brownies, sprites, elves, or spirits of nature, have been transposed through numerous legends and stories, changing radically during the Romantic period of the 1800s, both at the hands of illustrators and writers.

While Anglo-Saxon folklore was very precise in its definition of Fey, giving a name to every 'fey-like' manifestation, benign or malignant, which appeared in literature, in the collective imagination they were often identified as small winged creatures, eternally childlike with a capricious and happy character.

The link with nature and the primeval magic of the earth was conserved, while the Fey and elves hid themselves amongst 'large and stupid folk', a bit like we imagine a wild animal. There are also stories to scare children, the ogres and evil or cruel 'Fey': stories with children being substituted, and malicious pranks of disrespect. And yet all of this has created a coherent myth in continuous evolution that has expanded to as many cultures as those from which they originally derived.

When Mara began work on this splendid deck of Tarots she broke with the traditional 18th-century interpretations of Fey, however. The first question she asked herself was what they really represented and why. The answer that Mara has given through these 78 illustrations is the result of an interior and artistic quest, reaching world-wide.

The Beautiful Queen
The Queen of Wands here, while very similar to the final version, portrays an even stronger feeling of rebellion mixed with sweetness.

Study for the 9 of Pentacles
On her first try, Mara didn't quite get the lazy, spoilt attitude of the card.

Her Fey do not come from one place or one situation but roam the world and cross all ethnic divides as a testimony to the universal nature of Magic. Surprising in their more common aspects, they nevertheless carry with them an echo of what the joy of life is all about, and the links with nature and Magic from which their essence comes.

As such, they are truly universal Fey. They are not an echo of the Pre-Raphaelite 1800s, but a culture that still lives today, that dreams, hopes and exists; they evolved, adapted, and did not disappear to hide in the woods or rare oases. Mara's Fey live and dream… and while we are able to see them, even if only through the cards, they will live on.

The idea for the deck

The idea for the deck of cards came from Pietro Alligo, artistic director of Lo Scarabeo since 1987. Looking at some of Mara's drawings and illustrations in the comic book 2700, he immediately recognised this very young painter's latent talent. Mara was immediately interested in the subject of Fey and began searching for a concept and a structure, which then became the deck. From what I know of Mara's character, the Fey symbolised for her her unrestrained joy of life. Furthermore, her artistic formation is not Anglo-Saxon but Italian, while her imagination was nourished by Japanese 'anime' cartoons when she was young. She immediately identified the Fey with magic, joy, and that whole invisible world made up of happiness. While possessing extraordinary artistic sensitivity and an effective and clearly characteristic style, she totally lacked any esoteric culture and experience in the world of Tarot. For this reason I was asked to join

Rough 6 of Wands
Mara was just trying to see the composition and graphical balance of the card. Both the Fey expression and the nature of his mount were left blank on purpose and defined later.

The Queen of Dreaming
This black and white sketch shows even more clearly the ethereal, watery nature of the Queen of Chalices.

her and guide her in the creation of this deck, providing both a viewpoint for interpreting the Tarots and my experience regarding the esoteric aspects of the decks. Needless to say, poor Mara returned home that day burdened with books and selected passages on Tarot which she "absolutely had to read".

I remember the first time that Mara and I met to discuss the deck. We were at Caffè Elena, one of the historic cafés in Turin, talking through several beers each while the Turin evening proceeded around us along the River Po. It was a very informal meeting, but extremely productive. We talked for many hours about Fey, Tarot, and art, both of us involved in this extraordinary creative process. It was then, while Mara took notes by drawing and creating sketches one after the other, rather than writing anything down, that I vowed not to throw away anything that she did.

Luckily I didn't, as those sketches illustrate better than anything else what went in to creating this deck and arriving at the final version. They show the route that Mara, and I as her companion on this trip, took to arrive at the Fey Tarot.

And so Mara and I defined our respective roles: I became the wise mentor, full of knowledge and suggestions, while Mara was the young heroine, full of courage and energy, capable of arriving where I could not, thanks to her artistic sensitivity… but mostly thanks to her ability to communicate with a spirit that constantly tries and succeeds in perceiving.

Many meetings followed that first encounter, both formal, with hours of study in front of one card or one symbol, and informal, discussing perhaps Fey or the cards already made and forgotten about.

My role, in actual fact, was slighter than I would have wished. If my words give

Wind in the desert
The final study for the 5 of Swords.

The face of knowledge
Study for the face of the Seer or High Priestess. It is very difficult to capture an expression of timelessness and knowledge in such a simple posture.

the impression that the concepts behind each single card are only mine, then that is wrong and does a great injustice to Mara's strong personality. I was often only a spectator, a witness to her creations. At other times I was of help, but I am more comfortable in the role of narrator than of author.

The working method

I soon realised that in order to capture the best of Mara's 'poetry' it was necessary to leave her free without overloading her with a restricting script or with necessary graphic or symbolic elements. Mara was like a Fey, and needed to feel like a Fey while she painted these cards. Inspiration versus understanding.

Mara began working on the Minor Arcana, the suit of Chalices to be precise. We both agreed that often the minor cards are the most overlooked in a deck, whereas in fact they are the ones most in need of real pictorial characterisation. Her drawings became more refined and sure in stages and her perception of the subject also grew, as she entered more profoundly into the logic of a deck of cards, rather than just as single subjects to be understood individually. So it was better to begin with the aspect of the deck that was easiest for her and with which her spirit was in greater harmony.
The first stage was a generic discussion about the suit, its role and its overall significance.
Mara responded by choosing a chromatic tone that would be maintained throughout the suit to give it unity and enable immediate identification of the images. Colour, in Mara's designs, is extremely important because it is often a vehicle for her state of mind. Chromatically localising the cards that she planned

A valiant warrior
The trick in the 7 of Wands was to keep the image as flowing and as mobile as possible, without creating a comic book effect.

A devilish Pet
Study for the character of the Devil. In this sketch the creature is not at all frightening or destructive, but is almost 'cute'.

to create, Mara synthesised all that I had said regarding the basic similarities of the suits. The second stage was the definition of a meaning for each card of the suit. We then moved on to examine how that meaning was rendered or transformed in various Tarot decks.

At the beginning Mara ingeniously thought that there was a unique relationship between the card and its meaning. Each card has many meanings that are often nuances or facets of the original archetype. With man having created hundreds of decks of Tarots over the years, however, each aspect has been highlighted at different times or ignored at others. What Mara nevertheless tried to do, using me as a walking-talking encyclopaedia, was to match the meaning with the Fey as she saw it.

I realise now that Mara had, from the beginning, a precise understanding of the Fey and how she wanted them represented, much better than I did. It was a large topic, difficult to express in words but much easier to express in drawing, as she did.

From here on it was easy. Mara shut herself in her studio, in the shadow of Moncalieri Castle, to create her drawings. At times there were telephone discussions. After all I was the editor's 'long arm' and my job was to be her ally for Lo Scarabeo. Sketches, more sketches.... studies of details and expressions... until the right image was found.

For some cards Mara took half a day, for others the exchange of first drafts between us took over a week. The funny thing was, which I often teased her about, that even when the draft had been finally approved, her final version was completely different. Quite candidly, she would show me the print, as if an excuse, saying: "But it seemed so beautiful".

Mara's real talent when applied to the Tarots was her concentration in learning

Fey Expressions
Hair, eyes and clothing should evoke the character of any Fey at a glance. While humans change their clothes according to the situation, what Fey wear is an integral part of them.

Peace and fullness
Definitive study for the 9 of Chalices.

and her attention to detail. Often, during my work for Lo Scarabeo, I have encountered authors who were technically exceptional, but who paid scarce attention to the existence of the Tarots. For Mara, instead, the Tarot was the key. The drafts therefore were not an artistic experience but a search to understand the significance of the card (for this reason, in this book I will attempt to lead the reader to an understanding of the card's significance using the route illustrated by Mara's drafts and thus enabling the reader to follow the same path that the artist traced in her mind).

To the very end, therefore, Mara tried to improve each card, always attempting that unique combination between divinatory meaning, the Fey and their world, and the spirit of the painter.

When each suit was completed, the fearful moment arrived. Mara and I went together to Pietro Alligo, the artistic director of Lo Scarabeo, to show him the results of all this effort.

With a serious demeanour, glasses and a beard, he would look at each card in silence, turning the pages slowly, engrossed. Mara, meanwhile, would nervously talk and talk, indicating this and that in her drawings. Finally Pietro would say, always making fun of us: "That's good Mara, very good. We are very happy." Then the three of us would examine each card from a graphic and artistic viewpoint, looking for defects not to be repeated.

According to our plan, Mara should have completed this deck of cards in two years: in actual fact, three have passed. Meanwhile her career as a painter has begun, destined for certain success.

Often she broke off and took the opportunity to travel all over the world and Italy, and from each of these experiences she brought what she had learnt back to the Tarots. Artistically she grew and matured without ever losing the basic enchantment of her art: enthusiasm and fresh energy. It was a world without shadows, contagious in its vivacity, but full of perceptions, profoundly linked to reality and to experience lived in its essence and substance.

INTRODUCTION TO THE TAROTS

I would hope that the reader who has arrived this far is not totally ignorant of Tarots. For his/her eventual benefit, I will briefly introduce this fascinating world in order to provide the basis for a better understanding of this art and of these Fey Tarots.

Historical notes

The first historical mention of Tarots goes back to the first half of the 1400s in the courts of northern Italy. The first decks of cards come from that period too, and some of these cards have been conserved, especially the famous Visconti-Sforza deck, preserved almost in its entirety.
Just to give an idea of the age of Tarots: the Tarot existed before America was discovered.

One thing that is surprising, in that it is extraneous to what is commonly thought about Tarots, is that the original Tarots did not have any divinatory or cartomancy significance. Rather they were playing cards, for the so-called "ludus trionphorum", the game of Triumphs, which even today is played in northern Italy with few variations. That decks of cards existed for the general population is

The traveller turns his back
The first version of the 8 of Chalices had to be more detailed. The final version gained in depth of meaning, for it gives the idea of solemnity and silence.

Shards
In the final version of the 5 of Chalices the Fey gained much more personality and consciousness.

without doubt, given the historical documentation, even if, unfortunately, they have not been conserved due to the poor quality materials with which they were made. However, the decks for the aristocracy were produced in gold and silver and commissioned from the most famous artists and miniaturists. It is believed that the Visconti-Sforza deck was created by the pupils of Bonifacio Bembo, supervised by the Master himself.

Unfortunately, no historical source can trace the real origin of the Tarots and why they came about. There were definitely two distinct types of decks in the beginning, which were then united. The first was made up of a normal deck, named a "semi napoletani" (Neapolitan suits), which became the Minor Arcana (these are the cards from ace to ten, plus the Knave, Knight, Queen and King); the second was formed of 22 additional cards, unique to the Tarots, the so-called Major Arcana.

The renaissance, and medieval iconography

The Renaissance, as a historical period, was defined as such because the Western world awoke from the Dark Ages of the medieval period with a re-flowering of the Arts and the Humanistic sciences. Nevertheless the Renaissance owes a lot culturally to the medieval period, an era that was less barbarous than most people believe.

If we imagine an epoch where the greater part of the population was illiterate and uneducated, it is easy to understand how art was the primary form of communication. It is useless to write books if people are unable to read them. Better to

Material Fey
In the beginning, the Fey appearing in the 3 of Chalices were not composed of energy.

Blind Justice
In order to convey the frailty of Justice, the card was envisaged as a Fey child playing with sand on the seaside. However none of the preliminary sketches convinced. They all lacked the eternal quality of something higher than human Justice.

commission a fresco or a statue that the people can have access to and easily 'read', notwithstanding their ignorance. Thus in the medieval period a true alphabet of art was created that associated each concept (mainly sacred and theological concepts) with a symbol or an allegorical representation. Even the ploughman returning from the fields could recognise Saint Sebastian in a painting, Faith in a statue, or Geometry in a miniature, as can a modern scholar. These symbols and allegories were second nature to his language. It is not surprising, therefore, that playing cards were also invaded by these concepts and so the Tarots originated. The basic structure of the Tarot is an ascending order from the lowest (the poor Bagatto-Magician) to the sublime (the World), a 'cosmological' order that, if it was not part of the common philosophy of that era, was nevertheless sufficiently familiar and intuitive to be educational.

The production of Italian cards continued uninterruptedly for approximately 500 years, until the beginning of the 1900s. In the meantime the game became widespread throughout Europe, becoming extremely popular in France at the beginning of the 1600s. Here, for the first time, the drawings of what were to become the Marseille Tarots were created, deriving from a deck produced in Lombardy.

The Marseille Tarots

There are three main references in the history of Tarots - three iconographies, or three decks - which had such an important influence that they are considered fundamental. The first, in chronological order, is the so-called Marseille deck.

The stance of a Queen
This should have been the original Queen of Pentacles. But, even though beautiful, it was somehow out of character. It was therefore necessary to start anew.

"For Riccardo's attention"
Mara used to send me sketches by fax, so I could tell her to proceed or to change something. As you can see, the 9 of Chalices was slowing taking shape.

Blueprints of a fairy Chariot
This was the fax Mara sent to me explaining her idea for the Chariot. You can see that it's easier to see it, rather than describe it.

In the next page:

A Shakespearean Fool
A study for the Fool Arcana. It was still too lyrical to be a perfect Fool, but we were very near.

A feral Fey
The 4 of Swords seemed too feral. What the card had to show was commitment and inner conviction, not passion or anger..

In reality there are hundreds of decks that share the same symbolic and allegoric structure. The presence of a printing factory in the area of Marseille allowed the playing card industry to produce decks of greater quality and for less cost than their competitors. The diffusion of decks from Marseille was such that all over Europe the producers of Tarots rushed to produce decks similar to the Marseille type, following the fashion, to the point where the alternatives were all but forgotten.

The Marseille decks became standard for the game of Tarot and were also the deck that the esotericists used, firstly the French in the 18th century, to devise the divinatory structure that we still follow today.

Up until the 1600s the Tarots were not linked with cartomancy and divination. The cards were, however, often used to read the future - a widely-diffused practice in all levels of society during this era. Normal playing cards were used or else special decks called "Sibille", or Oracle cards, which were created precisely for divination. The structure of the Sibille cards was very simple: the card had an image and a phrase that gave it a meaning. The images and meanings were very practical and connected to common issues; they never mentioned speculative, esoteric or metaphysical issues. An example of a phrase from the Sibille: "Loss of money", or "young brown-haired woman, malicious and jealous". It is easy to imagine how these cards were used.

The Tarots, with their charm, unusual structure and the aura of mystery surrounding them, were part of this scene but not in a predominant manner.

The cultural impulse that came to identify the Tarots as an esoteric instrument came in fact from two other sources. The first was the fashion for Egypt and all things Egyptian. Travels, discoveries and archaeological findings, brought Egyptian culture to the West again, and it was treated with a mix of stupor and wonder. Hieroglyphic language was unknown at the time and contributed greatly to creating a sense of the exotic and the mysterious, to the point where anything that came from Egypt was precious and important… even, may it be said, ignoble fakes and worthless items. For esotericism, the Egyptian hieroglyphics became the 'language of magic'.

The second was from a renewal of Hermeticism. Many ancient Greek books and texts from the Hermetic culture were rediscovered, translated, diffused and

analysed. Even though this cultural aspect involved only a certain type of student, and not the whole of society as with the Egyptian fashion, it was nevertheless fundamental.

Between the end of the 1700s and the beginning of the 1800s, via the publications by the French esotericists such as Antoine Court de Gebelin, Jean Francois Alliette alias Etteilla, and Jean Baptiste Pitois alias Paul Christian, the entire world became convinced that Tarots were originally Egyptian and were an important instrument of Hermetic magic.

The Egyptian origin of Tarots. True or False?

False. All the archaeological and historical evidence that gave Tarots an Egyptian origin has been revealed as imprecise or clamorously false, and the conscious attempt to demonstrate, independently from the truth, that they were effectively Egyptian in origin, became more and more obvious. On this basis, all the researchers agree that the theories claiming an Egyptian origin for the Tarots are false.

But the real importance of this belief held by 17th-century esotericists did not lie in the truth or otherwise of their theories, nor in the honesty of their intentions: it lay in the fact that it was universally accepted and so successful that the tradition of Tarots was conditioned by it for almost two centuries. Even the controversial and genial Aleister Crowly called his deck The Tarots of the Book of Thoth, following this magic theory.

The Ace of Pentacles
The first sketches were almost unrecognisable from the final card. We can see the Ace coming from the hand of the fey, but in the Pentacles suit it was more important to have the Pentacle as an actual part of her.

Magic of the Moon
Study for the Moon Arcana.

Who are the great masters of European Esotericism?

My aim here is not to provide an exhaustive list but to cite at least some of the key personalities so that the reader has an overall idea of the history of Tarots, and might even perhaps direct his/her personal research.

- *Antoine Court de Gebelin.* Self-styled archaeologist, in 1781 identified the Tarots with the legendary Book of Thoth (god from the head of Ibis is the depositor of knowledge of the Egyptian religion).
- *Etteilla (Jean Francois Alliette)*, following the theories of Gebelin, corrected the Marseille iconographs, 'Egyptianising' and 'restoring' them according to the originals described in the Hermetic texts. He also altered the numeration of the cards.
- *Elifas Levi (Alphonse Louis Constant)* linked the origin of Tarots to the Caballa and to the Jewish Alphabet.
- *Paul Christian (Jean Baptiste Pitois)* completed the theories of Gebelin and Etteilla.
- *William Westcott*, founder of the Hermetic Order of the Golden Dawn, structured the esoteric aspect of the order of the Tarots, highlighting their magic aspect.
- *Papus (Gerard Encausse)* attempted to join the various forms of Western magic traditions into one coherent structure, among which the Caballa, astrology and the Tarots.
- *Arthur Edward Waite* identified the link between the images and their mean-

Dreaming the stars.
There was something touching about this study for the three of Wands, but the final version is powerful, and somehow more complete. Still, looking at this drawing one also gets a powerful impression.

An idea for a Knave
The Knave of Pentacles in an unfinished sketch.

ings, composing a precise iconographic legend for the Minor Arcana. The resulting deck, designed by Pamela Coleman Smith, is known as Rider Waite, and become the 'bible' of Tarots in the 1900s.

- *Oswald Wirth* gave substance to French occultism and in particular to the work of Papus in a deck which combined the Caballa, astrology, alchemy, and Massonic traditions.

- *Aleister Crowley*, with the spectacular art of Lady Freida Harris, published the deck of the Book of Thoth, still to this day the most hermetic and fascinating Tarot deck. The book that was supposed to explain the deck is however very difficult to understand.

At the beginning of the 20th century the history of Tarots moved from France to England, coinciding with the birth of the Esoteric Order of the Golden Dawn. The real importance of this event happened however when the Order divided into various confraternities and the secrets of the Tarots of the Order were made public on various occasions. The enormous amount of knowledge, studies and esoteric thought that up until then had been the dominion of a few, was in a short time, available to everyone. Even the Tarots themselves, with the Rider Waite deck, were able to be understood even by the uninitiated.

From a cultural point of view the event was phenomenal, and I believe substantially changed western culture. From that moment onwards, Tarots evolved

Sketches sent by fax
Final sketches for the 10 of pentacles and for the Emperor.

through various cultural movements of the 1900s, losing most of their magic and esoteric denominations, but at the same time acquiring immediacy and learning from psychology and from the encounter with oriental philosophy.

The Rider Waite Tarots

Of the three fundamental decks, the Rider Waite deck is the second in chronological order, and perhaps the most important. The reason for this is that it is simple and at the same time incisive. Thanks to this it is a standard and a reference point that all other Tarots must live up to. And in fact it is the most copied and the most studied deck.

I believe that the Rider Waite deck has as many limits as strong points, but nevertheless I cannot ignore the fact that it represents the departure point and the arena for confrontation for modern cartomancy. But it should not be the arrival point too, as this would mean that for 100 years we have not evolved at all.

Waite, the head of one of the branches of the Golden Dawn, approached a young illustrator by the name of Pamela Coleman Smith, who translated Waite's thoughts into images. This was 1910. The original deck was in black and white and was later coloured by an unknown person the following year, for publication. For technical reasons the cards were printed with colors without shades or precise borders.

This deck clearly brought about two innovations in the everyday use of Tarots (nothing that had not already been said; but it diffused, transmitted and made them easier to understand).

The first was that the meaning is connected to the image and this did not necessarily apply only to the Major Arcana but also to the Minor Arcana. The second

Studies for the 10 of Chalices
The first drawing is the detailing of the male Fey character, while the second is a study of the composition of the final card.

A face of Power
The face of the Emperor is seen from a different angle than the final version. The expression is indeed powerful.

was that each symbol and each element in the card has its own significance. Explaining these symbols and linking them to a pictorial interpretation, anyone was finally able to practice divination.

The Book of Thoth: the Tarots of Aleister Crowley

The third component of the fundamental triad of cards in the history of Tarots was designed by Lady Frieda Harris over six years of hard work, under Aleister Crowley's direction, and then published in 1944.

If the Marseille deck can be defined as 'traditional' and Waite's as 'symbolic', Crowley's deck can be seen as 'magical' or 'hermetic'. The cards are fascinating, above all the Major Arcana, and the artist was evidently inspired in their creation. The minor cards, in that they are the fruit of the same esoteric research, unfortunately do not express the same inspiration and are very deluding with respect to the earlier cards. Nevertheless, notwithstanding the difficulty in using and interpreting these cards they still remain incredibly fascinating and this attraction has continued to grow as, little by little, the tangle of indications provided by Crowley are unravelled by scholars.

From the artistic perspective

While in the historical camp I could flaunt my learning, looking at the Tarots from an artistic viewpoint necessarily means introducing a subjective component.

Cards of light that have never seen the light.
Forgive the pun, but these two cards were totally changed in the definitive Arcana.
The first should have become the 8 of Pentacles, while the second should have been the five of Pentacles.
Somehow, having a Fey caged to provide light and shelter to the other didn't feel right.

The question to be asked is: "what are Tarots?" If a simple answer existed this would be wonderful. The fact is that regardless of what certain authorities can affirm, there is no answer. And to each answer given it is possible to reply: "They are also that, among other things" (as an exceptionally good American cartomancer once told me).

For me, one of the principle aspects of the creation of a deck of Tarot cards is that of communication. The artist and the author (not necessarily the same person) try to communicate something to the reader, but, like a theatrical opera, the communication does not occur at the same moment in which it was created but is repeated each time the deck is used, with a different public but also with different actors, directors and scenography.

In this sense the job of whoever creates a deck of Tarots is not to provide the answers but rather to provide an expressive, not literal or linear, alphabet that can be interpreted each time.

And for this reason it is called Art. A scholar of Aesthetics (the science that studies Art), would kill me for such a banal definition of art, but I see it as the capacity to express via a means/method (not of a person but via a painting, a statue, a poem…) a sentiment, an emotion, a concept that cannot be controlled but that is entrusted to works of art.

In front of a work of art, the person approaching it is involved in a process of

Love and distance
Almost the definitive sketch for the Lovers card. The definitive card was much more synthetic and powerful, but the idea was already here.

The Ace of Swords
The ace is the first card of each suit and it is particularly difficult because the artist still has to 'get inside' the atmosphere and symbols of the suit.

stimulus and perceptions that leads him to understand something implicit within the work, even if it is an ineffable sensation.

According to this definition each card in a Tarot deck must be a work of art, because each time the cartomancer and the querent find themselves in front of a card they are attempting to find that well of meaning that the illustration alludes to. For this reason a list of meanings or keywords will never be a substitute for the art work.

Many of the greatest artists in the world have ventured into Tarot decks, even if the majority of them have never published or permitted publication of their works.

Such a quantity of references cannot but weigh upon an artist, but it is often precisely the bond with the significance of the card colliding with the need to say something personal, or with something that resonates with one's own spirit, that has created the most beautiful things.

To sum up, the art of Tarots is not decorative, but the main key for reading and interpreting the cards.

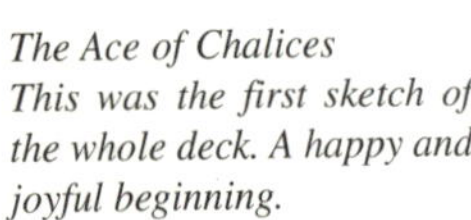

The Ace of Chalices
This was the first sketch of the whole deck. A happy and joyful beginning.

Judgement
And this was the last card to be completed. It was a 'Judgement' of sorts.
The sketch was too funny to be good, but there was a certain feeling which completed the deck. Actually it was more of a terrific emotion.

AND FINALLY... DIVINATION

Why Fey?

Magical creatures have populated western folklore for years, giving life to the legends of sprites, elves, gnomes, Fey… at times of sunny disposition, at times frightening, or even alien and diffident to larger folk. In different forms the magic is manifested in all cultures and in all places over this green land: Fey creatures, or creatures who are magical by nature and who live apart from the odious mould that the industry of man has imposed on the world.
Magic in fact, has always been connected to nature. From the Miyazaky's gentle "Tonari-No Totoro" to the Blue Fairy in Pinocchio; from Peter Pan to the sprites in the glades of New England. Are they real or fantasy? Regarding Tarots, it is better to think of them as symbols; symbols of a link with a world we are at risk of losing; symbols of a vital energy common to all, to each place and to every age. It is said that the Fey are visible only to the elderly or to children… but whether they are real is a question of faith. However, the energy they come from, whatever we want to call it, is real, and always true.
This is why these creatures have no master, race, creed or colour. They have wings because they are free. They have no age, because time for them runs backwards, and they show in their essence what they really are. This is their magic.

Strange arms
In this discarded sketch for the 8 of Chalices, it is possible to see how the nature of the Fey may be described through changes in anatomy and proportions. There is something fascinating in this Fey, even if it is not in accordance with the 8 of Chalices.

One of many
The final King of Swords is one of the most beautiful cards in the whole deck. This is just one of many sketches of the card.

The graphic realisation

Mara used different techniques to provide the atmosphere of each card, although giving a surprising coherence to the total work. This is a symbol of one of the characteristics of Fey creatures: variety.
Variety, coherence, difference, affinity. These are the important concepts that in the world of Fey are never in contradiction. In a world where form is the mirror of interior nature (as in the world of magic, where it is not possible to lie), appearance loses its significance, if it has not become a link with what we really are. The Fey therefore are young or old, big or little, coloured or human, grotesque, or elf-like. And the form that they take on, the places where they reside, are all echoes of the magic nature of the spirit of whoever confronts himself with the cards.

The Esoteric Structure

The Fey Tarots are a very precise magic pathway, closely linked to what can be defined as the traditional structure of Tarots. The wind has carried away the astrological designs (the Fey have little to do with the stars) and the cabalistic references (the intellectual work of man does not marry well with instinct and nature), but the indications that refer to life remain. They provide a parallel between what is in a card and an emotion or a recognisable sensation.
The Major Arcana can be seen as a pathway of illumination, where via 22 passages, man arrives at a greater level of understanding. The Fey, austere or joyous,

A different perspective
This version of the three of Wands is almost definitive. It was still necessary to understand the composition of the card and the final layout.

The 6 of Swords
Crossing the river of the world. In the end the concept was slightly modified, as this seemed too 'Celtic' in nature.

are guides and symbols for each of these intermediate passages. They are examples and reflections of the world from the other side of the mirror, from where we can look at ourselves.

The usual suits have been maintained in the Minor Arcana: Chalices, Pentacles, Wands and Swords. As an example, rather than filling the 10 of chalices with chalices, the preference was to make one chalice more beautiful and precious. In the Ace the Fey itself is the chalice (or sword or wand or pentacle) with its arms outstretched and crystal water from a spring. In the following cards this 'seed' which is planted in the ace grows and matures until it reaches its maximum potential.

Nevertheless, whoever is already familiar with Tarots will not get lost in the Fey Tarots and will find what they are familiar with using a language consisting of Fey images and symbols. They will also find something more, because the Fey have their own magic, but this will be discovered slowly, sweetly.

The **Chalices** represent the emotional and spiritual world. The Fey that run through these cards are dreamers, in love, sweet and sensitive. They receive and offer without fear or any vanity, demonstrating their open hearts without deceit; they are like clear running water.

The **Swords** represent the intellectual and conflicting world. They are wounded Fey, burdened by pain or responsibility. In the various images they show their strength and their vulnerability. They find a melancholy joy in things and an

An Internet search
It took a lot of time navigating the Internet before a good picture of a Lobster could be found to be used as a model for the Knight of Chalices' mount.

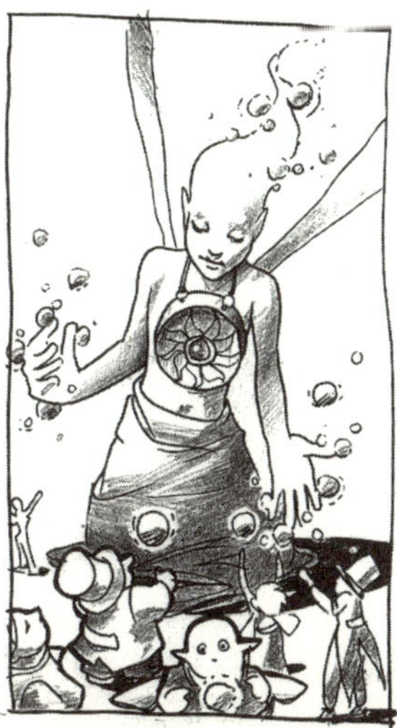

Giving
The original 6 of Pentacles was simpler and the composition less balanced. The final result was better adapted to the secondary meanings.

immense strength with which they confront the world, which can be terrible and dark for them too. Mara found it very difficult to get close to the Swords due to the disturbing feeling they emanate. There is however a strength and a joy in them much older than time itself that cannot be suffocated. The energies that guide man to do just deeds, to raise up his head in adversity and to deal with pain, are the same that animate their Fey nature. They are like the cold air that blows in autumn.

The **Pentacles** represent the physical world, the world of objects and earthly securities. The Fey that take shape in these cards are linked to the world that surrounds them, they are part of it and are often creators and craftsmen. They demonstrate the patience and immutability of real things and shun the castles of dreams, deceit and illusions. Their magic is real, physical and tangible. They are the earth beneath bare feet.

The **Wands** represent the world of man, what he does, feels, asks… Man, not that big clumsy being that we are, but man the individual, that graceful primordial spirit that resides in each soul. The Fey creatures that appear in the wands have the courage to fly, to choose and to act. They are not pushed by issues, necessity or by others, but place themselves at the centre of their world, and project what they are externally. They listen but never lose their identity; they are like the flames of a fireplace in the middle of a room.

The Major Arcana, however, are symbols of greater weight. It is very difficult to explain the relationship between the Minor and Major Arcana in a few lines. They are different, like night and day, but not separate. The Major Arcana looks at the Cosmos, the meaning of existence. The Minor Arcana looks at us, at the individual, at things close to hand. The Tarots therefore are complete only by traversing both worlds.

The first 7 Arcana govern the Material World, where the path of the hero begins, in a territory familiar to him (as has been stated previously the Arcana can be seen as a pathway from ignorance to illumination). The second 7 govern the World of Ideas, where the hero's journey continues to barren lands which he has glanced at but does not know. Finally the last 7 govern the Heavenly World, of the Answers and the Questions, where magic has its origins. The last (or the first) is the number zero, the fool, which is the beginning and the end of time, right and wrong, little or big, man or spirit. This card is the incarnation of all contradictions and defies any definition. It represents, in essence, the ordinary man.

The **Major Arcana** can be considered the heart of a deck of Tarots.
The greatest energies of the cosmos are concentrated in these 22 cards, or, at least, here these energies are described.
It can be observed how the Major Arcana, seen in sequence, illustrate a cycle of learning. It is called the Journey of the Hero, and describes the process of evolution, the growth that each spirit must achieve until completion and happiness. An initiatory journey that does not belong only to the 'great' or to great structures, but one that we live every day.
The nature of man is to search incessantly for answers and happiness: the first makes sense of our lives; the second because happiness is one of the most precious gifts. We realise early on that it is not possible to have one without the other.
The Journey of the Hero is a symbolic journey that man undertakes passing from ignorance and innocence to understanding and illumination. It speaks of things that we all know: joy, success, ambition, pain, laziness, fear, solitude, friendship, hope, redemption, courage.
In brief, it is a beautiful story. I believe it is very important to remember, in whatever moment or occasion when one finds oneself reading the Tarots, that the person in front of us is involved in this journey. And that this person is a hero, at the peak of a wave or at the bottom of the barrel, but always a hero trying to follow his path.

A two-step journey to true wisdom
Two different sketches for the King of Wands. It was going to be a child, but was the child playful or wise beyond his years?
The first image is the introductory sketch, while the second is the definitive one.

MAJOR ARCANA

Briefly

The Fool

The Fool is anyone who has no perception of himself. Therefore he moves with a lack of awareness and in ignorance, looking elsewhere for the answers he already has.

He remains a blank board and an unexpressed potential, that could transform itself at any time.

The Magician

The Magician is whoever tries to change the world. He accepts responsibility for his actions and for his choices. He soon discovers, however that it is not so easy and begins a long journey to learn.

The Seer

The Seer is the guardian of the threshold of the conscience. She does not only gather all that a man could need to know but above all describes the processes of learning and of study and research. She is a friend, but to receive her favours always costs effort.

The Empress

The Empress is the earthly mother, governess of the world. Contained within her are the links with the femininity of the universe. She knows how to use intuition to decide; she knows how to fight with the heart; she knows how to use her own doubts for listening to others. She grows things and cultivates the world like a garden.

The Emperor

The Emperor is the earthly father, master of the world. Through him the masculinity of the universe is expressed. He knows how to make decisions when faced with necessity; he knows how to sustain the weight of things, and is reliable and present when needed; he looks ahead and fights with courage and consistency to protect what is dear to him.

The Wise One
The Wise One is the spiritual father. He knows how to balance wisdom and knowledge, power and ability together. He complements the Seer, since they are a couple: the spiritual mother and father.

The Lovers
The Lovers represent a union of opposites, an understanding of things which are not made to be alike. Also the courage and the sweetness of this contact.

The Chariot
The Chariot represents success, glory and honour. It signifies the ability to take the things one needs and to dominate its surroundings. But the chariot also contains the limits to these actions.

Strength
Strength represents the real strength which can be drawn upon to face the impossible. Any difficulty can be overcome and in every moment of desperation one realises how strong one is. Strength is courage and discipline.

The Hermit
The Hermit represents the ability to live with oneself, to try and mediate, the ability to be alone and not have need of others. It represents the wisdom hidden in all things.

The Wheel
The Wheel represents the need to bend to fortune, the idea that things change for the better or for the worse and that when it is lost, it can be substituted by a new thing, incessantly.

Justice
Justice represents the presence of order in the Universe and the understanding that everything, us included, is regulated by this. Justice puts us in touch with pain and with the need for pain and sadness.

The Hanged Man
The Hanged Man represents contact with a different world, the proof and diffi-

culty in finding things that are not easy; difficulty in obtaining things, insatiable curiosity.

Death

Death is the beginning and the end. It indicates how ephemeral things are. In death we rediscover surprise, change, transformation: the capacity to leave behind certain things in order to proceed.

Temperance

Temperance indicates cure and healing; the moment when things are no longer important but silence and contemplation are appreciated. Here is a refuge for excesses and great deeds, in order to dedicate time to smaller issues.

The Devil

The Devil indicates temptation, failure, fraud, false illusions. It indicates a loss of judgement because one is blinded by needs or from arrogance.

The Tower

The Tower is the destruction of certainties that gave shape to reality. But these certainties, traumatic as their fall is, are also the prison that covered and closed every exit.

The Stars

The Stars are hope and infinite tension. With the stars one gets used to looking ahead and seeing the end of the journey.

The Moon

The Moon is a land of mysteries, of dreams and of intuitions. On this terrain it is difficult to distinguish the real from the illusory; even the greatest secrets and the greatest intuitions are conserved.

The Sun

The Sun is the card of security and of strength. The light of the sun illuminates everything and does not leave shadows or uncertainties.

Judgement

Judgement represents the culminating moment when all things find their result; when the truth is separated from the false and vice-versa.

The World

The World is the conclusion of the hero's journey. Each cause is united in a harmonious and present time. Each cause finds its meaning, significance, happiness.

Brief notes on the description of the Arcana cards

The description of the Major Arcana is divided in this manner:

The Sentence
A sentence that encompasses, often in a cryptic form, the elements of the significance of the Arcana.
It is important to begin with a sentence because this helps not to trivialize the infinite nuances of each card; rather it opens the door, the possibility, to intuition. To study the Arcana correctly, one is advised to briefly meditate on this sentence before continuing with the description of the Arcana.

The Image
The image is a description of the card. The elements that are part of this are extracted and delineated without judgement or symbolic interpretation.
The image helps the reader look at the card and teaches him to find the meaning from what he sees and not from what he knows.

Simple Meaning
These key phrases indicate a series of primary and secondary meanings that a beginner reader can use. Given the extreme synthesis of the keywords, a beginner should ask himself why the card has these meanings. This process is the first step in becoming an expert user of the Tarots.

Advanced Meaning
This part of the description highlights elements on the card and their relationship, together with their significance, whilst trying to note the nuances and the reasons for that meaning. Above all, this description helps put the card into perspective with those surrounding it.

The Chosen Symbols
This part of the description indicates in a schematic manner the symbols and the elements present in the Arcana and their relationship with the overall meaning. Often an analysis of the symbols can lead to greater understanding of the Arcana; however one should never limit oneself to the symbols in describing the cards.

Reflections

Here the personal reflections of the author are inserted, comparisons with other decks, with other Arcana, with personal iconography, and all that is still to be said but did not find a space previously.

O - The Fool

The Sentence

Ignorance, like doubt and uncertainty, are the basis of human nature and of the pathway towards wisdom.

The Fey that governs the card of the Fool is the Fey of many beginnings and of quest.

Just as an empty container can be filled, a blank page covered in writing, a question formulated to have an answer, the Fool indicates the emptiness of knowledge and of trust that can take shape and be reclaimed.

This card indicates the immense universe of the "it is not" and the "don't know", of things yet to be done, to be thought or to be understood. Those who "don't know" can be both noble princes and simple fools.

The Image

In a blue sky, with clouds or mist, the Fey Fool rises. His dress is divided into green and violet because his instinct is to push in different directions, often against each other. His eyes are like pools of emeralds, full of ancient wisdom, yet still childlike, as they know nothing.

A crown dominates his forehead, but contains a lock which is still closed, behind which are all his thoughts and knowledge of the world. In one hand he raises a pumpkin, carved with a grim and crude face, from which emanates a light that reflects on him. His other hand is turned towards himself, as if to ask a question, just mentioned from his half-closed lips.

A golden belt tied around his clothes holds infinite keys of strange shapes, some old some new, some big some small, some precious some cheap. Amongst these keys is without doubt the key that opens the noble casket of his mind.

Simple meaning

Lack of direction, madness, strangeness. Questions without answers, paths less trodden, mental games. Distance from the truth, simplicity, ingenuity.

Advanced meaning

In the older tarots the Fool was he who did not believe in God and was therefore excluded from his grace. Later on he became the one who walked on the edge of the precipice, not being aware of the abyss that surrounded him.
In the world today, full of answers and certainty, the Fool is the incarnation of a thousand questions, doubts and uncertainties. He always carries with him an undiscovered wisdom and an unexpected courage and humanity.
Often when the chosen card is the Fool, it is a time of confusion and doubt, but not evil or obtuseness. Just as we were all once children, the Fool recalls that part of ourselves when we knew nothing and looked at everything.

The Chosen Symbols

The crown indicates each person's potential, the knowledge and the spiritual strength of one's being.
The pumpkin indicates dependency on others, conformism, external quest when we should be asking ourselves.
The coat of two colours signifies how man's nature and thoughts are rarely coherent and concentrated, and how we often have to live with opposites that never mix.
The keys indicate the choices that man can make, and his profound and unalienable liberty.

Reflections

The Fool is identified by the number zero. It is not before nor after any other card. It is free, and outside the scheme. There is a random potential in this card, not to dominate something but to remain always free and not be subordinate to any law. The Fool is always the beginning and the end of any quest or journey.

I - The Magician

The Sentence

Will is what leads man forward on his journey towards understanding; to learn to act and to bend reality to do what he wishes and desires. The Fey that presides over will has abandoned any ambition within himself. He is moved by joy and not by pride.

He has observed reality and in the real art of magic trusts his desire to change things. However there is no malice or domination over other creatures.

The Magician begins the journey towards knowledge with an infinite thirst to learn and to try everything. He traces life, like the hand of a blacksmith feeling the metal under his fingers, a painter preparing colours, or a mother raising her children.

He has great power in his hands, and yet it remains a small echo within the universe.

The Image

In his own place, the Fey that incarnates the Magician has reunited the four elements that comprise the world. In a chalice he has collected the red nectar of all the emotions. In a sharpened dagger he contains the wishes of the Wise Ones to divide, comprehend and indicate. In a disc of precious brass he has enclosed the perfection of each thing brought into existence. In an ancient plant, though small, he has placed the desire of each thing to grow and live.

Humbly on his knees, he places himself before his real family, and because he bends down he is not large in either dimension or consequences, but important, and this requires a lot of attention and detail.

The mouse is white, since all elements are in its light and its eyes are red, twins to the fire that shines in those of the Magician. Above the Magician a lamp of a thousand lights becomes faint in front of the power of the Magician.

And here, between his hands, while a smile widens on his young face, is the image of the creature that will be created. It is still a reflection, an echo of the great life, because the Magician cannot substitute the force of creation, but it is already coming alive and moving its tail.

Simple Meaning

Will, magic, power, control, ambition. Quest, study, creation of man.

Advanced meaning

The Magician represents the first card on the journey towards 'illumination'. At one time he was enriched with frivolous things and the smallness of his figure, but the tarots of the last century transformed the Magician into a courageous man attempting the quest for the secrets of the cosmos, and therefore gave power to this card.

On the Magician's card, the four symbols of the suits are present, as forces of all types meet and balance in this figure. For this reason the Magician is the representation of will. Only through his intervention and his control of magic can these forces run together and create, without losing themselves in confusion.

The Chosen Symbols

The chalice, the disc, the sword and the tree recall the four suits and the four elements. The Magician draws from every force for his magic and bends all of the forces to his will.

The books indicate how the power of the Magician has its roots in tradition and in wisdom and does not come just from him alone.

The Familiar (a spiritual attendant, here in the shape of a mouse) indicates the wonder of the world that the Fey Magician is in touch with. This is reality.

Reflections

The Magician also signifies the man who brings his spirit before great and immense things. He needs to have great ambition and great courage to dare place himself beside Nature, and for this reason the road he travels is dangerous. If he realises his intention to dominate and covet things, his road will be short and treacherous. Only with the real joy of creation and of learning can he overcome the perils of pride.

II - The Seer

The Sentence

The doors that lead to understanding are numerous. The Fey that guards these doors is called the High Priestess and protects all that is, was and will be. Her eyes move patiently and her long hands trace words in an ancient language. To guard and to preserve are her roles so that the wisdom of the Fey is not lost. All those who are looking for answers, and know how to ask with courtesy, turn to her, because it is difficult to learn real wisdom.
The Fey Seer is the lady of the threshold and guards its opening and closing.

The Image

The Seer sits on a staircase of stone suspended in the heavens. At her back a simple door leads elsewhere. A simple glance cannot reveal what is to be found on the other side, nor guess it, unless the door is opened. On the door the symbol of time is inscribed, as knowledge has no limits. The Fey holds a heavy book on which shines the glyph of infinity. Her hands interrogate the knowledge that is contained there, while her grave and severe face is turned towards knowledge. At her back two stone dragons guard the threshold that separates ignorance from knowledge. One of these comes to life and, like playing a game, twists his head to be able to read behind the Seer.
A veil covers the back of the Fey's neck and whoever looks through this will recognise the difference between reality and illusion.

Simple Meaning

Study, knowledge, learning, concentration. Quest, gift of intelligence, wisdom, sensible judgement.

Advanced Meaning

The Seer (or High Priestess) is known in older tarots by the name of "Papessa" and signified Faith. For the ancients, Faith was to give oneself to God and therefore to reach an understanding of the revelations and the truth.

The process of learning is always a threshold, preceded by a stairway. The climb is hard and difficult but the reward is great. The Fey of knowledge sees into the present, as well as the past and the future, and dispenses the wisdom she knows, because only a strong heart understands how to carry the weight of knowledge. The dragon indicates that often the road towards knowledge is full of simplicity and curiosity.
For many reasons this card also indicates the truth. At the top of the interminable stairway, the veil of illusion and of deceit disappears.

The Chosen Symbols
The stairway represents the difficulty that needs to be overcome to learn.
The stone indicates that truth remains constant and does not change.
The sky indicates the solitude that one brings to these places, in that knowledge is personal and each person must walk the road in his own time and manner, in accordance with himself.
The hourglass indicates time and the mastery that knowledge gives over the time that runs.
The sign of infinity, on the contrary, indicates how time has no meaning in front of the Spirit.
The dragons are the guardians of the door, pillars that need to be crossed before passing over the threshold.
The books are infinite knowledge.
The veil is the illusion that separates the reality of the Spirit from the perception that we have of the same.

Reflections
The Seer is a card closely connected to that of the Wise One. In other tarots they appear as the High Priestess and the Hierophant. She has therefore a strong female nature, and at times is used to indicate the love that is born not from flesh but from respect and esteem. If one observes the timeless face of the Seer, it does not look cold and hostile, but almost sad, because things pass and she can do nothing to keep them. And yet her profound eyes do not look with ill-feeling towards the dragon, who in his ingenuity draws closer to her book.

III - The Empress

The Sentence

The dominion of the earthly world is governed by an alternation of the powers. Just as the moon rises and then falls and as the day becomes night to return dazzling tomorrow, the Empress governs half of the dominion of things. She governs between earth and sky. In her arm, strength; in her face courage, in her bosom she cares for and loves all things that are born and grow. She is mother and mistress; the infinite generative force.
The Empress is power born from life.

The Image

Tall, white towers stand out against the sky. Interminable forts and bastions, but with gardens at the top of the pinnacles, which are covered by trees and grassy pathways. All this immense fortress is the Empress's throne. She wears no crown but a simple thin headband of gold, and no other ornaments apart from two bracelets of ancient wood and stones the colour of her eyes.
She does not hold a spectre in her hand but has a puppy in her lap. This animal lives only in the world of the Fey and is the symbol of the Empress. Its fur is golden like the rays of the sun at midday; the horn on its head represents purity; its wings signify liberty and finally its powerful paws give it force. Nevertheless it is still small, embraced within the Empress's loving arms.
The Empress does not look at the things nearest to her. She is free, in command, and sweeps the horizon and the future with her glance.

Simple Meaning

Protection, courage, defence, guard, maternity, care, generations, fertility.

Advanced Meaning

The Empire, or rather the responsibility to command and govern can be handled alone if the Emperor or the Empress, the male and female principles, are in agreement. If this occurs, the earthly world benefits greatly and is at peace. The power of the Empress is nevertheless very different from that of her consort. As a woman she possess the capacity to raise things and to protect, and her world is rich and blooms. It is not surprising that she is seen as a Mother Goddess, but she is also a counsellor and as strong as the ancient mountains. Her expression however shows that she is not a servant but rather knows how to look ahead and to think of herself too.

The Chosen Symbols

The towers indicate the material world, the events and the things that occur to men. They are her throne and dominion.

The gardens indicate life and the immense vital force that emanates from the Empress.

The golden band indicates a queen's royalty but also the simplicity of her mission.

The winged unicorn indicates the attributes of power: purity, liberty, strength, justice. It is still a puppy, since the Empress is the force that generates and raises things, a morning strength, not of the evening.

Her coarse wooden bracelets show how the Empress must at times be a warrior and these link her with the earth.

Her glance turned to the horizon indicates that she is free from all things and does not serve anyone.

Reflections

Two concepts find harmony in the card of the Empress: the act of governing and femininity. This first of all leads to the generative force in the maternal womb, but is not limited to this. It is not glory or vanity that she looks for, nor to be the submissive figure at the heart of a family. She is a giant, immense and free and audacious, whose glance embraces the world. There is the strength in her to move mountains, but this is not aimed at war but at creation and the care of all small things.

IV - The Emperor

The Sentence

The Emperor is lord of the material world. The sun at its zenith crowns his head, as all things respect his wishes.

He completes the Empress and is completed by her.

His arm bears certainty and inevitability. He is the incessant guard, the tireless vigilant sentinel of the world that is entrusted to him. He looks across the hills and woods, eyes and flesh at the heart of things. He exercises his dominion guided by necessity and need, not by ambition.

The Image

The master of all things is seated on a throne suspended in the sky. The throne is rough stone, engraved and eroded by wind, not by artisans' hands, but it is admirably adapted to his figure. No crown adorns his head, because the sun that reflects on his face surrounds him with light. A three-pointed crown is engraved on the throne, a little above his erect head.

The throne, in as much as it is solid and heavy, floats in the air, raising and levitating the lord above everything.

Decorated armour covers his body - back, chest, arms and legs - but his gaze is fixed on the sun in front of him, without vacillating or hiding.

On a rock to his left an unsheathed sword is planted, which indicates the power that his arm brandishes. On his right, on another suspended boulder, is a winged unicorn, symbol of his command and the link that he shares with his consort.

Simple Meaning

Command, responsibility, guide, leadership, management, trust in power, authority, administration, empire, dominion, security.

Advanced Meaning

As with the Empress, the Emperor possess only a part of the dominion. Only if he governs in harmony with his consort will there be peace and well-being. In

this card, as in the previous one, the missing part assumes a power equal to that present, until both are present.
In the heart of the Emperor is the masculine principle of dominion and of government. He is more distant and cold, more aristocratic and powerful, but his face is equally young and beautiful.
Pride is one of his defences, as the burden of command weighs on his shoulders and he is always ready for war and conflict. He would like to descend from his throne but cannot until his job is completed. He is the Emperor and Father. He keeps watch on the world from on high.

The Chosen Symbols

The stone indicates the link the Emperor has with the earth.
The roughness of the inscriptions signify that the dominion of things has been entrusted to him from Nature and not from his subjects or from his power.
The stone, heavy as it is, is free in the air indicating how the dominion of the Emperor in the material world is born from the spiritual and the mental world.
The three-pointed crown imprinted in the stone recalls the three worlds: material, mental, spiritual. The branch higher than these three points is the limit of the lord's power.
His armour indicates how the lord Fey is the shield of the world against evil. The sword is the power of the Emperor, now appeased and at rest, but always ready to move.
The winged unicorn is the symbol of his power and of the love that links him to the Empress.
His white eyes that do not close in front of the sun indicate that he is not afraid of the truth.

Reflections

Comparing this card to that of the Empress, his coldness emerges. Where everything with her was sweet and warm, here it is bitter and crude. This is the masculine nature perhaps, to be at a distance and to be more preoccupied by abstract and invisible things rather than the grass that grows beneath tired feet. For this reason the Emperor and the Empress have need of each other if the Kingdom is to prosper. Where she uses instinct and intuition, he possesses wisdom and intellect. Where she acts out of love, he acts from necessity. The roots of their love are profound.

V - The Wise One

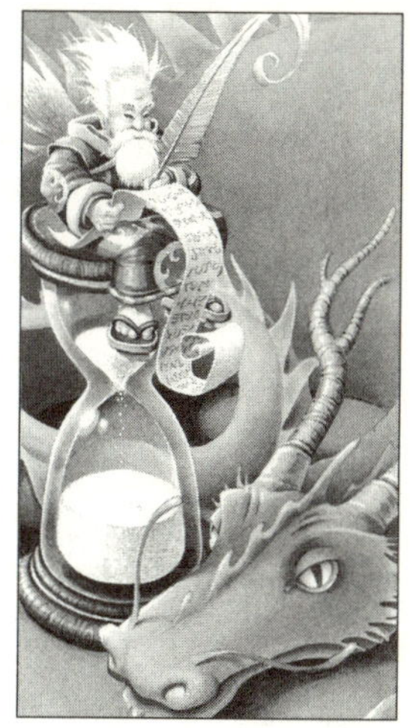

The Sentence

The Wise One is the custodian of the wisdom of the heart and the wisdom of the Spirit. It is said his room can be found on the other side of the threshold guarded by the Seer, because he is the intermediary between the material and the spiritual worlds. His words are comforting and calm; his virtues are wisdom and patience.

Of all the Fey, he is the one who has decided to accept time that passes, to grow old and vanish. But this has freed him from time and has given him the heart to see each thing in the present.

A venerable and wise creature, he is the source of infinite, ancient and wonderful memories, of experience and advice. He has learnt great things over time, and has fathomed the abyss of knowledge at length in order to learn.

The Image

In a room where the walls cannot be seen, there is a strange chair in the shape of an hourglass, within which the sand runs, slowly yet inexorably. The body of an immense and powerful dragon occupies the entire space. Its branched horns are the symbol of a great magic force. Its eyes are veiled and half closed, overcome by sleep and resignation for his companion. On the hourglass sits the Wise One, an elderly and minute Fey. But he is the king of the Spirit. On his forehead lies a third eye, now closed and no longer used, since the time his normal eyes and his gentle heart have allowed him to discover other souls. He is dressed simply and intent on writing with a long quill from some magical creature.

Simple Meaning

Wisdom, advice, experience, suggestion, ritual, rite, comprehension.

Advanced Meaning

The Wise One is the Seer's consort. For this reason the symbol of the hourglass recurs in both of their cards. However, if the link between the Emperor and the Empress was one of communion, that between the Seer and the Wise One does not lead to them meeting, as their roads are diverse. Where she is a custodian, he bestows freely. His house is made to answer and to guide, to divide the wisdom that he has gathered.

With the Wise One, one has to return to the heart in order to reach the Spirit, and there find all the knowledge that cannot be learnt from books, but only from things that are made and experienced.

Furthermore, one needs to understand one's limits and accept the things that pass, keeping every memory intact, however.

The Chosen Symbols

The hourglass indicates the passing of time and the sin of hesitating uselessly.

The Wise One's great age, his white beard and bushy eyebrows indicate how time is not an enemy but in fact allows things to grow.

The roll of parchment, lined with his writing, indicates that experience can be shared and given and that there is much to be gained from listening.

The closed eye in the middle of his forehead indicates the capacity to examine the heart and to see other than material things in the world of the Spirit. His eye is closed because he does not need it now, in his peace as a Wise One. Not all powers need to be used always.

The dragon indicates immense power, sleeping: the great power that the Wise One controls and can draw from.

Reflections

This card, also known as "The Wisest", introduces a guide. He has the great qualities of the elderly and the venerable, and also their defects. It requires great patience to interpret his wisdom and to get close to his advice.

Again this card talks of time and reminds the Fey that a right time exists for everything, and likewise for beautiful things or things of great value: they need time to arrive at last and to bloom.

VI - The Lovers

The Sentence

To meet, even in diversity; to choose, even in doubt; to love, abandoning oneself to the heart and to life.

The present moment is not the past and not the future, yet it embraces them both. Man does not come from the Earth nor from the Sky, yet his spirit is attracted and composed of both.

There is no need to be afraid of the differences or to choose between them, but to perceive how each thing is completed by the other.

The Image

A spring from a rock rises towards the sky, and the clouds lower and draw the air against the stone.

A male creature made of rock and earth, with strong gnarled hands like the roots of a tree, sits between the rocks. A female Fey made of dreams and air, impalpable and light, hangs without substance like a pallid form through which the light shines.

Their hands are joined in their hair, in a caress that is at the same time love, a promise, comprehension and intimacy.

Simple Meaning

Coincidence of opposites, love, harmony, union, permeation, comprehension, tolerance. Choice, test, difficulty, separation, desire attained.

Advanced Meaning

The card of the lovers in ancient times was given the job of harmonising and reflecting on the differences that there were between virtue (a chaste and courteous lady) and vice (an immodest lady, already gone to seed). Love could address the attraction of the loins (material) or the attraction of the eyes (spirit).

The choice made in this card is similar to that of Adam and Eve in the garden of Eden, when they learn for the first time the difference between good and evil.

In the lovers the accent is placed on the harmony of opposites. As in the Tai Chi

Tu (the Taoist diagram), only harmony between extremes gives peace. And this is also a profound anthem to love, because only great love can ensure that the earth and the sky are together, always attracted, and always rejected.
Not surprisingly the ancient Egyptian legend of the creation of the world recounted that each thing was born of the union between earth and sky.
Therefore, prior to having a sexual or carnal component, the Fey Lovers are the symbol of all the diversities that need to be filled, the different languages to be translated and the steep ravines of the spirit, the body or the mind, that need to be crossed by bridges.

The Chosen Symbols

The earth indicates the things that last; the air, that which changes.
The earth indicates material things; the air, spiritual things.
The earth indicates the body; the air the mind.
The earth indicates the masculine nature; the air, female nature.
The caress is a gesture that for an instant unites all, rendering it one.
Their eyes have the same soul.

Reflections

This card is first of all a card of love, either towards a partner, a child, or a friend, but its significance is deeper. Often each one of us is torn by conflicts between contrasting sentiments and sensations, very often between the needs of our spiritual nature and the contingencies and necessities of material life.
The card of the Lovers once indicated the need to choose. However at times there is no need to choose but to conserve both opposites, in peace.

VII - The Chariot

The Sentence

Run fast, on roads and bridges, crossing the earth, prey to haste, to reach a place in time.

The Fey that runs with the chariot is sustained by her magic and from this magic velocity and purpose comes. Willingness, knowledge and wisdom, dominion and power, all come to nothing if a purpose remains unmoved and is not guided or held by reins.

The reflections of triumph and success are in the river that the chariot crosses, but it has already passed by.

The Image

An arched bridge curves over a deep, swirling river. Around the bay the Fey chariot runs at great speed. The wheels are bent at strange slanting angles and the structure creaks, but the chariot does not slow down. A seated driver, holding onto a short platform, incites his steeds to hurry.

The body of the chariot is made from a sweet pomegranate, on the crown of which sits a Fey on a light green cushion. Her dress is warm, cheerful and elegant, as if she is ready for a great ball. A large autumn leaf acts as a parasol and protects her from the hot rays of the sun. Notwithstanding the speed and the crazy drive she does not feel the wind and is seated peacefully. Two steeds, by nature different one from the other, pull the chariot-throne. One is a small country mouse, with bright eyes watching the road, the other an emerald green lizard with a splendid long tail.

Simple Meaning

Travel, route, victory, triumph, conquest, ownership, vanity, displaying oneself.

Advanced Meaning

In the cards from past centuries the icon of the chariot had two different aspects. On the one hand it was a chariot of war, formidable and cruel, while on the other it was a chariot of triumph, on which the victorious leader sat, crowned with laurels to return home. Two sphinxes hauled it, one white to symbolise good and the other black to symbolise evil.

In the world of the Fey the vanity of men does not exist. The chariot returns to its original nature, that of transport and of movement. Each journey of the Spirit begins with a material voyage. And yet this magical pomegranate that overcomes obstacles also indicates the roof of the world, success and glory, because he who sits on top remains unchanged by things rushing around him, protected and at the centre of everything, visible and crowned with glory.

But this glory remains and will always remain in the world of material things, because this is its magic, just like the fairytale of Cinderella, the beauty who rode in a similar carriage to a great ball.

The Chosen Symbols

The river indicates traps and unknown dangers.

The stone bridge indicates the road made by others that we can follow, and indicates the security of the route and the direction.

The pomegranate indicates the sweet fruits of victory.

The mouse indicates good, or perhaps bad. The lizard indicates good, or perhaps evil, as in each journey there is a bit of one or the other and it is not easy to distinguish them.

The driver is the guide that we give to our actions. Using him, the good and the bad of things follow the same road and arrive at the destination.

The cushion is the comfort and joy of being lead ahead.

The autumn leaf is like a crown of glory that protects and shows the way.

Reflections

A card of movement and audacity, it shows intention. Without aims or desires, man is as empty as a deserted road. But if he gives his real nature a direction, this acquires form and each step brings him nearer.

Without purpose of action, man is lost, passive, waiting, but in the Chariot this waiting ends and he comes to the road.

VIII - Strength

The Sentence

The Fey who makes a display of strength will be neither great nor powerful, because true strength is not shown off. Strength hides from eyes and laughs, while standing up to enemies and subduing them.

There are no secrets behind strength, as it is clear like a mountain stream and raging like a rocky waterfall. And yet, even though there is much strength in those hands, they would count for nothing if the arms and fingers did not also know how to be gentle.

There are many things to deal with, some insidious, but many great, terrifying and powerful. There is always a need for strength.

The Image

A minute Fey, dressed in the skin of a strange magic animal, has just won a battle against an enormous dragon-serpent with many heads. At her side shines the hilt of a sword almost as big as her, which has however remained in its sheath fastened around her slim waist. Her eyes are limpid and clear and her mouth is cheerfully smiling. Her shape is still immature, adolescent and childlike. On her head, from a hat made of fur, horns and tusks emerge like ornaments, from wild beasts more dangerous than the one she has just captured.

In a tangle of shapes and spires, ensnared by a long thin rope, a terrible monster struggles in vain: part-dragon, part-serpent, with numerous heads. The child warrior has seized it firmly by the tail and ignoring its protests and its enormous weight, she sets about taking it away.

The monster's eye is not angry or evil, but stupid and defeated by the courage of its enemy and by its own impotence,

Simple Meaning

Courage, force, energy, constancy in adversity, triumph against a superior enemy, the triumph of good over bad, justice against falsehood, reason against brutality, laughter against silence.

Advanced Meaning

The origin of the icon for strength showed a young girl opening the jaws of a lion, a simple representation of the force of reason and intellect against that of instinct and brutality. Whether the enemy is within us, or outside, strength is always the good that defeats the bad: Saint George who slays the dragon; Thor who raises the serpent Midgard from the earth…

In the world of the Fey, Strength is important, and the Strength Fey is a true invincible warrior. But she is not calculating, nor does she possess any cruelty. Just as once the young girl infringed the jaws of the beast with her purity, the strong Fey does not brandish a sword to stop his enemy or dominate him.

Strength also means an outlet for joy and energy from apathy and from the silence of weariness. It means finding lost things and never giving up. It means trusting in good and in oneself; feeling sure when things seem terrible that it is only a small thing in comparison to the resources of the Spirit. Above all, it means courage and trust.

The Chosen Symbols

The Sword indicates the limits of strength. According to the oriental masters a real warrior never kills. For this reason the sword remains in its sheath, even though carried by great Strength.

The tusks in the hair indicate that this enemy is not the first and will not be the last.

The rope, which is very like the tail of the dragon-snake indicates that evil often turns on itself.

The two heads show how evil never comes alone and that everything needs to be faced to win the duel.

The dimensions of the Monster indicate the terror that obstacles place in front of us, and how fear is often the real enemy.

The seizing of the tail shows that the evil of today can be dominated and become part of the strength that we will have tomorrow.

Reflections

Until the beginning of the 20th century, Strength was the eleventh card, then different decks exchanged it with number 8: this was the sequence followed for the Fey. The card that is now number 11 is Justice, also a Fey child. Perhaps Justice and Strength are not so far removed from each other.

IX - The Hermit

The Sentence

A lost Fey is looking for the path. He finds himself in the place where all the lost and forgotten things are gathered. There is doubt and guilt, but also memories and joy.

The light shows the shadows and the routes that lose themselves elsewhere. But it is the light of the Spirit that illuminates the way and that keeps us safe from any danger.

The Fey who searches, wanders in solitude, but he is not afraid because he will find the way.

The Image

A labyrinth of many shapes on various planes, of a confusing and impossible geometry that winds in every direction. Within it there are abandoned stairs, doors and hidden, secret spaces.

With careful but sure steps a slender Fey opens a road in that maze and looks for the direct path. His tall hat holds a gem like a silent third eye, and he extends his arm towards the darkness to distance it.

Strange and timid creatures live in this forgotten place, but they do not flee when faced with the light of the Hermit; they use it to observe for the first time the features of the place they live in and to marvel at its secrets.

A closed book is placed on a ceiling-floor, just hidden from the view of the searching hermit but within the circle of his light.

Simple Meaning

Solitude, research, meditation, exile, obscurity, reflection, silence.

Advanced Meaning

The Hermit has chosen to separate himself from the other Fey and to reach the crossroads of infinite possibilities. Here it is easy to lose oneself in the darkness of lies, doubts and fear. But the Hermit does not hurry and moves his feet slowly. He is looking. Not for light, because he brandishes that and with it removes ignorance, but for something else, which he keeps in his heart. There are many roads but he never gets lost. It is difficult, however, for those who wish to follow the same road. It is necessary to immerse oneself in things hidden, lost or forgotten, and risk losing oneself for something precious that was mislaid. Where all other lights fail, the Hermit is there to guide us, in solitude, to give strength when there is fear, a safe guide. In part it is our conscience that emerges when we are lost and alone. In part it is the guide who inevitably arrives to save us when we are lost in a hostile place.

The Chosen Symbols

The doors indicate the infinite possibilities and the infinite paths that open before us at any time.

The stairs indicate how the paths rise and fall and it is not always the downhill path that reaches the valley.

The creatures indicate those who are lost and are agitated without a guide in the darkness of solitude.

The book indicates the hidden treasure that is concealed within everyone.

The eye gem that is on his hat indicates the need and the desire to search and to meditate in solitude.

Finally the lamp indicates the light of the Spirit that shines strongly when we are alone and that guides us in our choices.

Reflections

The Hermit is a card of solitude. It is not, however, a mournful and gloomy exile from company elsewhere but rather a reflection of those roads we must travel alone, and those answers that must not come from others. Growth, as we learn from infancy, whether spiritual, mental or even physical, is at times painful and dangerous, but necessary and rewarding.

The Hermit therefore is the card of internal quest and growth of the self.

X - The Wheel

The Sentence

Everything turns, time turns the seasons and the alternating fortunes of man.

The wind turns and destiny turns, and everything is created and falls apart. Nothing in the material world is forever. But once the loss of things is accepted then new things are born and change and evolution is accepted.

The Image

Like two children intent on playing, two mysterious Fey are seated on the floor of an old room.

The first Fey is young and impatient, with a sweet face and untidy hair. A belt of spring flowers is tied around her waist and she is lying over the top part of the spiral wheel.

The second Fey is elderly, with long white hair gathered in a bun behind her head. Her face is serene but severe, and autumn rests on her clothes. She is sitting quietly behind the wheel.

The Wheel, an immense spiral, stretches between the two Fey, beginning from the centre. It is made of trees, objects and animals, like a game, but it is the wheel of the entire existence, in the hands of the two kind Fates, Norns or Parcae.

The first hand builds and creates, widening the spiral, little by little, irresistibly, but the second hand takes pieces away and places them to one side with the same irresistible speed. The wheel therefore changes shape and substance without ever moving. The piece that was placed to one side returns to the design and is again removed.

Simple Meaning

Time, cycle, change, metamorphosis, chance, changing fortunes, rise and fall, success in things.

Advanced Meaning

The wheel, the supreme card of circular symmetry, shows the alternations and vicissitudes of life.

What is made is destined to be destroyed, and when it is empty it is time to be refilled with new strength and new energy. This dance is not obscure or gloomy, but silent and yet full of joy.
Within the wheel, space can be found for destiny, and for acceptance that things go as they must. There is also space for the realisation that after many bad things it is inevitable that good things occur, and that once the bottom has been reached one must inevitably rise up again.
It is a small warning against pride because everything that we have as opposed to what we are is not eternal and sooner or later will leave us.
Last but not least the wheel contains the running of natural time, the seasons that follow one another and then begin again, just as the earth revolves around the sun, orbit after orbit.

The Chosen Symbols
The luminous leaves indicate spring and its creative force.
The young Fey indicates the freshness and spontaneity in creating and giving.
The elderly Fey indicates the solemnity and severity in taking and in ending.
The three-fingered amulet represents the three Fates, or Parcae, from ancient mythology.
The rosary belt around the waist indicates the memory of all things that pass.
The toy houses indicate things, objects and minerals.
The toy plants indicate plants, places and vegetable matter.
The toy animals indicate life, nature and animals.
The spiral wheel indicates the eternal expansion of the spirit.

Reflections
In antiquity, the Celtic population were subjects of the Roman Empire and made offerings and blessings to the three Fey, who were no other than the three Fates, or Parcae, who safeguarded destiny. For the ancients, destiny was a thin thread that unwound and was then finally cut. Leaving aside the meaning of this card, one thing to ponder is how time works on the Spirit. All things pass and yet the finger of time has not touched the most profound part of what it is to be human.

XI - Justice

The Sentence

The Fey of Justice is a child Fey. What eye could see the truth, beyond any deceit? What mind could support the weight of decision and choice? What hand could hold the heart of man?
Justice gives order to things and gives them meaning. Without consequences, each act would be useless and justice is the force that links each cause with its effect.

The Image

There are many doors, arches and pointed windows lost in the confines of this immense room. The child Fey is pale, like ivory under the light of the moon. Her skin is smooth and there is no sign of wrinkles. Her hair is white and braided, leaving her forehead clear and showing her large white, trusting, but blind eyes. A painted third eye shines on her forehead, because she does not lack her senses. However, what her eyes can fathom is not what others are able to see. Between her outstretched hands a suspended feather shines, extremely light in the immobile air.
The child Fey is nude, clothed only in heavy gold jewels: they tie her plaited hair, decorate her neck in a golden yoke, and encircle her arms in a heavy gold bracelet.

Simple Meaning

Justice, necessity, responsibility, consequences of an action or an event, what must be, what must happen, discovering the truth, revelation of a deception, compensation and punishment.

Advanced Meaning

Justice is not the law. That belongs to the material world while this is the justice of the Spirit. All things have consequences and it is not for us to say what is right or wrong for others and to judge them.
Nevertheless it is the road we take that leads to punishment or reward, because this is the nature of things. When the card of Justice appears it is because that moment is near, or at least right.

There is a great and profound innocence in the Fey Justice, since her heart is empty of malice and pure as it was at the beginning of everything. Free yet a prisoner, as her load is heavy. She has sacrificed her own sight to be able to see beyond.

The Chosen Symbols

The many doors indicate the shadows and false justice that try to confuse issues.
Her white skin indicates the solitude and isolation of the Fey (like the seers in the temples in ancient times).
Her blindness indicates a lack of attention towards material things, which others maintain to be of importance.
Her third eye indicates second sight for things that are eternal and that are really important.
The feather indicates the heart of man being judged (in Egyptian mythology Anubis chose the worthy by weighing their hearts against a feather. If it was heavier than the feather they were condemned).
The heavy ornaments are the glories that chain us. They are the links between the ethereal and the abstraction of justice and the material world where this is applied (they were inspired by the ornaments and jewellery used by West African populations).

Reflections

Justice is the fulcrum that gives order to the universe. Placed in the exact centre of the deck, the number 11 gives meaning to things. If there was no superior order nor any spiritual justice (removed from any ethical characterisation), all would be chaos and disorder.
Furthermore, Justice is the first card that is connected to the spiritual world and not to the material world.

XII - The Hanged Man

The Sentence

When two worlds are turned upside down, one within the other, when what appears strange becomes normal and what was normal becomes strange. This is the Fey of the Hanged Man, the Fey of the upside-down.

The Image

In a profound abyss in the ocean, where there is no other light except that from a distant surface, a few ancient ruins from a forgotten people emerge on sands, undisturbed by any currents.
Fish of every size and colour inhabit this place and all turn with curiosity towards the intruder from the surface. They swim to him without threat, in silent questioning.
The hanged Fey is holding a stone dolphin which is depicted while frisking above the water. Head down, legs crossed aiming at the surface, but his arms are anchored in a new grip. His face is contracted from lack of oxygen, as this world is strange and hostile for him and he would not be able to remain here for long. Yet he resists and his eyes draw close to the largest and boldest fish.

Simple Meaning

Difficulty, trial by ordeal, sacrifice, change of perception, meeting different realities, moving to a different or superior understanding, understanding diversity, noting something that was hidden although visible.

Advanced Meaning

It is not easy to immerse oneself in the depths, in apnoea, holding one's breath for sufficient time. Yet it is the only way to enter into contact with another reality, to understand different languages and forms.
The hanged man, without renouncing his own world and identity, has dived into another world, with the intention of understanding and discovering. Just like that, with his head down, he is a bridge, a link, an umbilical cord between the two worlds.

And what he discovers is not so strange. The fish are not enemies or indifferent, and they look at him, also curious and friendly. Although it is difficult to hold his breath, he has discovered, in the eyes of a much feared enemy, the same look of understanding and friendship. The dolphin statue that he grasps is the second part of the link. Perhaps the dolphin is also upside-down, symbol of great intelligence yet without hands or works, but above all a symbol of the inhabitants of the sea who emerge and dive into the air.

The Chosen Symbols

The ruins indicate the mystery of the things we ignore.

The upside-down positions indicate how we need to alter our perceptions at times and to put our heads down.

The contracted cheeks whilst holding the breath indicate the fatigue, the difficulty and the inevitable transitory nature of this condition.

The eyes meeting indicate a possibility for translation and understanding among ourselves and different cultures.

The dolphin indicates that other forms of intelligence, even though diverse, can open our own minds.

It also indicates how the dolphin is 'hung' in the water, with respect to the air.

Reflections

In old decks, this card indicated a terrible ordeal, an initiation rite to reach greater understanding. The Fey do not have crude habits like those of man. There remains however a strong desire to see each place and thing and to surpass the limits. The difficulty and the fatigue pass, but what was observed while the head was upside down remains with us.

With the number 12 this card is balanced between the world of the spirit and that of the intellect, and therefore rarely refers to an exploration or a physical fatigue.

The dolphin also recalls one of the artist's soft toys that sleeps on her bed every day.

XIII - Death

The Sentence

In the end the principle. Death appears dark and black, terrible beyond the veil of our thoughts. When reached, it has a kind face, however, welcoming in itself. She is the Fey who has lived only once.

In death there is transformation, a passage. The end of the present moment, now past, is the beginning of a future moment, now present. It arrives suddenly, inevitably… yet like a friend long courted.

It is not the death of the body, nor that of the spirit: it is an obligatory passage, a metamorphosis.

The Image

She has two eyes of different colours. One indicates hope, and shines with light, where any other kind of light would not show. The other shines with an angry and dangerous light, because she is the great consoler from whom you cannot flee. Her face is kind and rested. She gazes with a friendly smile, patient and at the same time sad because of the fear she knows she inspires. She rests her head in her hand, waiting without haste for the last move to be made. Around her neck is a medal that shows an eclipse. The moon covers the sun and hides its light, precipitating the world into an illusory night.

She sits at a round table where a circular chess set is shown and a game is in progress. The Star has fallen and the white king is frozen with fear in the centre. The black pieces are menacingly surrounding him: towers and wheels, justice and wisdom and finally the world. At her back a single egg is hanging from a thin thread, the only ornament in this room.

Simple Meaning

End, termination, surprise, transformation, improvised things, unpredictable, inevitable. Longstanding fear, rest, dark, blindness, transitory moments, metamorphosis. A new beginning.

Advanced Meaning

Death, as the name declares, is the card that frightens and terrorises. On many occasions the most common desire of those who reflected on this card was to distance themselves from the shadows and flee from the omen.

But in the world of the Fey nothing can really die because the spirit is immortal. Yet Death attends the threshold just the same. Things end, get lost and disappear. As an eclipse hides the sun's light, death describes all the times in which we emerge from the dark, before being immersed in another light.
It is therefore the metamorphosis and the transformation that occur and not the end itself. What we knew disappears. We need to recall that death does not give weight to status, riches, power or glamour. There is no announcement of its arrival. Yet nothing is left unchanged.

The Chosen Symbols

The green eye indicates hope and the red eye indicates danger.
The medal shaped like an eclipse indicates the dark and therefore the return of the light: the transitory nature of death and at the same time the fear that it induces.
The circular chess set shows the relevance of everything.
The chess pieces indicate other cards in the tarot:
- the white star is the Stars and the symbol of hope that vacillates;
- the white king is a King and a symbol of a man who has reached the end of his path;
- the black tower is the Tower and is a symbol of the threat contained at the end of everything;
- the wheel is the Wheel and is a symbol of rebirth and the passing of time;
- the dragon is the Wise One because when afraid there is need for advice;
- the angel that blows the trumpet is Justice and a promise that death is not the end;
- The snail is the world and indicates how everything is not completed until it has reached its own end.

Reflections

The face of Death was greatly influenced by Sandman by Neil Gaiman. When this card was still in progress I asked Mara to give it a face I could fall in love with.
Nature has worked so that beautiful things do not induce terror and that in the beauty of the spirit there is deep promise and great trust. This card represents change in its novelty, in its hope and promises and also in the fear that it creates and in the uncertainty of not being able to see beyond it.
The egg, indicating life and fertility, quotes from a famous painting by Piero della Francesco, the Pala di Montefeltro. This alchemical symbol, in a central position in the painting, was specifically requested by the Duke of Urbino as a lucky omen for his wife.

XIV - Temperance

The Sentence

Water, air, earth and fire sparkle together. Not distinct and separate but together. Not united and alone, but singing with different voices.
The Fey who cures, who heals, who mitigates and dilutes, appears after the night. She is the dawn Fey. Hers is the soul that soothes wounds and torments. Memories fade and lights are relit.

The Image

Everything that is within temperance brings silence with it. The veil of water ripples lightly and its confines are confused with the beautiful, silent sky. Without making a sound the Fey turns her head towards the right and moves her hand lightly. Around her forehead is a crown of live fish that swim in synchrony, maintaining their distance like dancers. But their fins plough through air not water. The Fey's hair is lose and wavy in a silent, discreet wind. She wears two golden jewels in the shape of a circle as earrings. On poles of wood and shells, planted in the earth and just below the water, small braziers are barely visible. They emit a white, odorous smoke, as if from the centre of a temple.

Simple Meaning

Soften one's approach towards others, care, rest, refresh, recuperate energy, quiet, silence, sweetness, lose oneself in passion, patience, receptiveness, attention.

Advanced Meaning

The original icon of Temperance showed an angel that mixed water and wine in two carafes, to dilute one and to improve the other. Here however the four elements, though never evident, noted but vague, are nevertheless distinct and present: earth that provides sustenance and is perceived from below; water that meets the sky; air that lightly moves the smoke and fire in the braziers.
It is easy to imagine the silence and quiet of this place because it is also a place

for cure and rest, where wounds heal and the mind finds peace and tranquillity. Like a temple or a hospital, things move slowly and are never improvised, while the sweet smell of incense fills the air.

The Chosen Symbols

The air indicates trials and mental conquests.

The water represents the continual flow of the emotions.

The fire is man's energy and will.

The earth is the element that supports everything, even though it seems buried.

It was important that the four elements did not appear too evidently but were rather vague and just noticeable, without disturbing the quiet of the card with their presence. The quiet indicates restfulness and peace; the total absence of noise and violence.

The fish indicate life and its care and preservation.

The halo indicates the interior force that Temperance symbolises.

The braziers indicate the gratitude of those who are healed.

Reflections

It is difficult to convey sounds in an image, but it was very important for this card to do so. It indicates the life that begins again after death, the awakening from a bad dream or a long period of obscurity. It also indicates purification prior to beginning, in a holy place where fatigue and labours are abandoned.

XV - The Devil

The Sentence

An enormous beast, guided by its voracious instinct, devouring everything around it until nothing remains. A stupid beast, enormous and cowardly that eats, consumes, devours and does not understand. This beast can do no more than remain alone in a desert of ashes.

The Image

An enormous giant of fire and clay burning in the forest. Immense and curved horns adorn a huge head where little fiery eyes shine without intelligence.

Its features are brutal and its lineaments are bestial.

It constantly carries entire trees, still green, to its mouth, which it devours whole, while crawling on all fours; with the other hand, it uproots them from the ground. Wherever it has passed bare earth and leaves remain.

Simple Meaning

Burning passions, instinct, impulse, lack of reflection, stupidity, lack of foresight, myopia, brutality.

Advanced Meaning

The devil incarnated, evil, danger. The evil is however more a lack of judgement than malice or spite.

The beast has lost its Fey nature. The fire that it makes is its terrible hunger and without aim or design it continues to eat.

The evil turns against itself. As much as it could possibly appear to be beautiful it remains a greedy and voracious beast, simple and instinctive, that has drowned its spiritual potential to satiate its hunger and its impulses.

The Chosen Symbols

The fire was chosen as a symbol of strength that needs to be fed in order to remain, and for its destructive characteristics.

It is also a symbol of the guiding instinct.
The tongue is greediness and incessant, insatiable hunger.
The trees are the beautiful things that the beast crushes in its stupidity.

Reflections

The devil in its many forms is seen as evil, either dangerous, treacherous, ferocious, cruel, deceiving or tyrannical. The evil in a spiritual sense is that which distances us from the growth of the spirit. It is avid, lustful, greedy, proud, slothful, angry or jealous (the seven cardinal sins)… but in the end it is just incapable of looking beyond and realising the value of things.

XVI - The Tower

The Sentence

Things that were made one day are no longer. In as much as things can be trusted to time, it will devour them slowly and make them disappear. This is not a cause for anxiety, but of understanding the ephemeral, because everything vanishes; this does not mean it was in vain. The Fey closed in the tower watches the foundations of her house collapse and accepts that the world, today, is greater than her, and laughs.

The Image

A never-ending tower descends from the sky. Its foundations are not on earth but in higher and more secure sources. Its feet, those of an ancient colossus, are crumbling and open the way for the inhabitants of the air. Bit by bit the tower falls apart and abandons itself to the sky. From a window, a Fey who lives in the tower watches it collapsing while looking at the world below. Soon the barrier that divides her from the rest of the Universe will dissolve and she will be able to fly free.

Simple Meaning

Imprisonment, closure, ruin, arrogance that comes back on itself. Destruction of something, collapse of certainty, of habits, of confidence. Defences that fall, walls that shatter, doors that are flung open.

Advanced Meaning

The tower returns to the difficult concept of pain and of loss. The basic symbol recalls the ancient tower of Babel, where the will of man was opposed to divine will and man was obliged to learn his limits. Over time the tower has become a symbol of imprisonment and pain. On the one hand, it means withstanding the violence that infringes our spirit, like rocks against the waves. On the other hand, it symbolises the erecting of barriers and fortresses that protect from the outside, and seeing them finally fall.

There are moments when everyone needs to hide in a tower, to be closed within oneself and one's things, but these moments must pass, and man must know how to return to the cycle of life, to give and to receive. The moment, when it arrives can cause problems if one is not ready… but in the end it is necessary in order to continue growing.

The Chosen Symbols

The quadrangular, rather than circular, tower indicates the artificial nature of the construction and its difficulty in harmonising with the rest of the world.

The cloudy sky indicates the possibility of an evolution, either good (serene) or bad (storm).

The teradactyls indicate our fear in leaving the tower and at the same time indicate that the empty sky is actually inhabited and alive.

The Fey at the window indicates that it is necessary to accept the knowledge of collapse.

Wings allow the Fey to fly.

Reflections

The tower is drawn in such a way that it appears to come from the sky and not from the ground. This is because the foundations of man are always spiritual, not just material, and the force of time is unable to corrode that. All that we posses, even in terms of friendship, love, understanding, and health, can be placed at risk, but what we really are is untouchable.

XVII - The Stars

The Sentence

Stretching to infinity. When the world sleeps and every fear is left behind, when eyes are raised in the terse night and infinity is perceived… to observe, to hope… one understands for a minute with total clarity what it is that one wants. The sensation of being able to skim over the world and to change everything. A smile… simple, personal, aimed at oneself. And if someone saw it in that moment they would say "a star is born".

The Image

A balcony of moon-silver stands out above a sleeping world. A breeze envelopes the Fey Star, and she inhales the nocturnal fragrances. Her eyes are closed but continue to see the vault of the heavens. While the wind blows her hair, body and clothes, all her being tends towards infinity. From her, little stars are born, grow and leave the group; of resplendent silver, they throw themselves upwards to cover the entire sky.

Simple Meaning

Hope, foresight, guidance, a good story, intuitive security, a delicious awakening, immense personal joy, comprehension of the indescribable, beauty, innocence, future.

Advanced Meaning

The stars have always been guides for navigators; points of reference and direction. They influence man from far away, shining like points of light on a serene night.

For this reason they are symbols of hope. The ability to look towards infinity and towards the sky, and to gather, even if only for a moment, all of the infinite possibilities that are opened before us. Even if stars do not seem of great use as such, they nevertheless provide direction. They do not help us move towards our objective but they help us understand where we are going and why.

They are also the card of beauty, of innocence and of purity, because these are the characteristics of the soul that contemplates, even a little, infinity, and knows how to replenish, to have hope, joy and security. Watching the stars is like falling in love.

The Chosen Symbols

The white light is the colour of purity and of innocence. Evil never reaches here and will never be able to touch the Fey Star.
Nudity indicates turning towards infinity with all of one's being without veils or go-betweens.
Closed eyes remind us that we are dealing with a personal and intimate experience.
The outstretched finger, arched neck, and body posture indicate the intensity of the experience.
The stars that are generated from the body and rise skywards are the beauty within each creature, reflected in the beauty that each person is able to see outside themselves.

Reflections

It is often easy to observe the beauty and joy of others or in things so great that one feels insignificant in comparison. Nevertheless, each time we observe the beauty of something, whether in nature or in a work of man, art, poetry or person, a reflection of one's own beauty can be seen. This is not easy to realise; the stars are also this.

XVIII - The Moon

The Sentence

Docile note of power. Hear the little sister of the skies who talks and whispers of ancient mysteries. The hand of the Moon Fey moves to this song and traces the secret signs. The invisible is transformed into the visible and what was known disappears, covered in sand.

The Image

In a desert with no name, the moon shines huge and white yet non-threatening, giving a spectral pallor to everything. Forgotten stones of temples rise from the ground and the Fey, searcher of dreams, raises her head to listen to the soft song of the moon. Her hand holds a pole with a lunar scythe at the top, held as if to reap the moon itself. The other quickly writes in the sand the signs that come to mind, guided by instinct and by the suggestions of place and time.

Simple Meaning

Dreams, illusions, intuition, the worlds of the invisible, magic, female power, the hidden side, the receptive side, the soft side, the silent side, quest, transformation, inconstancy, capricious.

Advanced Meaning

The Moon is the Arcana parallel to that of the Sun. In remote times, the moon, was always connected with magic and female power. When the sun stopped shining and normal men went indoors, priests and sorcerers officiated in secret under the eye of the sky: the moon. Even today the moon contains infinite mysteries, like a civilization buried under the sand. The Moon Fey is a sorceress, powerful and sure, who moves alone, following only her Mistress and her instinct.

The essence of the moon is so magical that at times it does not seem to be connected to reality, almost like a mantle of illusion and inconstancy that wraps around its being. In this space, dangerous if one does not have sufficient strength to resist the allure of the night, the most beautiful feelings can be found, the craziest things never seen before, the shame never spoken of, the sweetest and most unreal desires. The real difficulty, as sorcerers know, is not to enter this place but to leave without losing oneself and abandoning oneself to being unsubstantial.

The Chosen Symbols

The full moon indicates the moon's great force, its maximum potential and pale splendour.

The huge moon, close to the earth, indicates its weight in matters and the energy that can be got from it.

The bent pole indicates the inconstancy and transitory nature of the world of dreams and of the moon.

The point with the lunar scythe indicates that man must turn to the moon and not abandon it.

The white body indicates how the Moon Fey is used to the pale heat of the moon rather than that of the sun during the day.

The clothes are those of a traveller and of a seeker.

The circular jewels recall the lunar disc.

The little sticks she writes with have no tips, indicating the instinctive nature of her gestures.

The signs traced on the earth show a moon and a sun together. A pale light seems to shine from them.

The ruins in the distance indicate both the allure and the fear of the dream world.

Reflections

Once again the Sun and the Moon meet in two worlds, masculine and feminine. They do not fight or oppose one another in any way. Rather they divide the day and the night. There are spaces where the moon rules and the sun is only a memory, and other spaces where the sun is the only light and the moon is slender, waiting.

Only with this reciprocal harmony for the other's space, can male and female beings possibly grow. Due to the nature of the moon, it is also a mystical Arcana. It is futile, even in bad taste, to try and rationalise its significance too much. The moon is instinct, intuition and nothing to do with reason or common sense.

XIX - The Sun

The Sentence

Light inundates everything and shows up every lie. Light eliminates shadows, fortifies the heart and drives away the cold. Light makes crops grow, and provides food, strength and health. Light is life.

The Image

A young Fey, with a body burnt brown by the sun, sits in a field the colour of gold and is nourished by the rays of the sun. The clouds redden with gold and everything is dazzled and nourished by the light of the sun.

Simple Meaning

Truth, courage, sincerity, security, certainty, strength, joy, power, glory, light.

Advanced Meaning

The exact opposite of the Moon, full of contradictions, the Sun is an Arcana that by nature is without any kind of ambiguity. It has no shadows, no veils, no half-measures. The light of the sun inundates everything and has no rivals. It nourishes, heats and protects. The sun represents all truths, all certainties, all practical things, all understandable things. It represents masculine power and the joy of fullness and of security, when no doubt troubles the soul.

The Chosen Symbols

The sun, luminous and fiery… paling slightly with the haze from the air.

The clouds receive warmth from the sun like everything else.

The golden wheat bends in the wind, reflecting heat from the star like a sea of molten metal.

The Sun Fey, dressed like a young farmer, with almost reddish skin, is wrapped in this light like a mantle. Rejoicing in the heat and the peace, more than the light, abandoning himself to the coolness that comes from the earth.

Reflections

The sun is an extraordinarily positive card; however, it is worth remembering that too much light is not good. Man is made to alternate between dark and light, security and doubt, truth and ignorance. The sun, if it did not give up its place at night, would burn and destroy everything instead of nourishing it.

XX - Judgement

The Sentence

When the moment arrives, there is no time to turn back, to recommence, to make things better. Everything will be displayed, every card overturned, every consequence dealt with, every responsibility concluded.

The sound of the trumpet awakens the traces we have left and will announce what we have done.

This moment is the boundary.

The Image

In a world that is not that of the Fey, the head of a creator lies asleep on a page. Her hand still holds the pen that is closing the knot of infinity. The Judgement Fey, white and transparent, sounds her trumpet and the spirits of all things rise and show their nature.

A T-shirt, a pullover, a pen, the ink, the drawing, the page, change into Fey, who are made of pure colour.

Simple Meaning

A moment of proof, responsibility, the consequences of past actions, reward or punishment, reawakening of the spirit, of dignity, of knowledge. Breaking down barriers or walls thought to be invincible, rebirth, obligatory passage, necessary battle to reach an objective.

Advanced Meaning

In its oldest form, this card represented the Universal Judgement. An archangel blew a celestial trumpet and the dead rose from their tombs to be buried or saved. With the Fey this concept of guilt, deriving from Christianity, does not exist.

Judgement indicates that there is always a consequence to our actions. Nothing is ever definitive, but each thing, each and every action we undertake, has its weight and responsibility attached: it leaves a sign. The Arcana of Judgement indicates that in the end this sign always returns to whoever generated it. There is nowhere to flee. It is the magic of the world… without which, even if at times it is annoying, we would not be happy, never be worth anything, never have a conscience.

The Chosen Symbols

White walls were chosen since white does not influence other colours but leaves them unchanged. Thus the Judgement Fey is white. She is ready to welcome but does not carry within her any moral judgement or prejudice. The Fey are of one colour only, because they are pure essence.

The symbol of infinity that has been drawn unconsciously by the artist's sleeping hand recalls the Arcana of the sorcerer. The cycle is concluded.

Reflections

This card is the only card that does not represent the world of the Fey. Although she denies it, I am convinced that this card represents the artist herself, in her studio. For Mara, the Judgement card meant completion of this deck, after three years of devoted energy. In dreams, when the conscious mind is not present and vigilant, the confines between the world of magic and the more mundane world become hazy. The Fey are within us, in everything, in each object that we create and that we touch with passion. Judgement also indicates how worlds are linked with each other: we do not need just to look at what we see to find a sense of harmony in things.

XXI - The World

The Sentence

Everything is composed of many parts, yet it is also something whole. If it is divided it loses form and substance, but when it really whole it becomes something totally different than the sum of its parts: it is complete.

The Image

This is the universe and it includes galaxies, stars and planets. Immense in this universe, there is a snail, on whose shell rises a mountain....on the mountain a castle, on the castle a tower, and at the top of the tower a dragon.

Simple Meaning

All, completion, complementarity, the comprehension and union of opposites. A good end, joy, happiness, peace, serenity. A prize, communion with what surrounds one, the spirit of the world. Water and wind.

Advanced Meaning

The World is the card that contains everything. This completion is extended to material aspects, to intellectual and spiritual matters, to everything. And all of the distinct elements which compose it are in harmony with each other. It is difficult to think of an Arcana that is more positive, stronger or more indestructible than this one. Precisely because of its completeness, the World also represents contact with the divine and the need to harmonise one's energies, desires and actual abilities in a unique space.

There is an old Japanese fable that describes the world supported by four elephants on the shell of a turtle that travels through infinity. The world of the Fey is a world of magic, of courage and wonder, where things exist without needing a reason to be. A world made of substance.

The Chosen Symbols

The snail carries the world like a house and reminds us that the world we live in is alive and moving. It proceeds slowly but constantly through the universe, which is even greater.

The mountain, the castle and the dragon all indicate living things, constructed things and things that are outside man's control. They are also symbols of the intellect, matter and spirit.

The circular geometric shape indicates the relationship between things and the cyclic nature of existence.

Reflections

In order to look at the world one needs to be able to remove oneself from individual perceptions. Each individual Fey is lost when faced with the complexity and the impressiveness of all this, especially when together. Nevertheless, the conquest of knowledge, the journey that began with the Fool, ends with the World. Here it is possible to reach infinity (not in the same way as with the stars, which are perceived for an instant), to have it at your fingertips: not to 'possess' it, but to 'be' it.

One of the most beautiful concepts repeated in this card is that whilst being a part of the whole, each single part is also the whole. A little contradictory according to Aristotelian logic, but nonetheless a key concept to understanding the beauty of this Arcana.

THE MINOR ARCANA

The Minor Arcana is divided into four suits, each having their own characteristics. The traditional suits, derived from the cards of the Italian Renaissance, are:
Chalices
Pentacles
Wands
Swords

In English, the names of two of these suits have undergone a radical transformation over time and in the evolution of the Tarots. Originally, Pentacles were called "Coins", but the English tradition has changed their name to Pentacles. In the same way, Wands were originally called "Clubs", instead of the current, more magical Wands.

In general the Minor Arcana are considered subsidiary or 'inferior' to the Major Arcana. The latter refer to the principles of the cosmos and of existence, great forces of epical proportions. The Minor Arcana however have a more practical and concise value.
Normally they refer to events, people, sensations that are closer and less abstract, linked more to reality as it is normally understood. To use a grammatical paragon, the Minor Arcana are like adjectives to the Major Arcana.

This is particularly important not so much for the study or the interpretation of each single card, but rather for the total overall vision of a card. The focal points are indicated by the Major Arcana while the Minor Arcana fill in the spaces, providing context and substance to the structure. With a little experience this division comes naturally and becomes a useful instrument for divination.

Until the beginning of the 20th century, the Minor Arcana were not illustrated in the Tarot decks. Only ten swords were presented in the card the Ten of Swords, or eight chalices were shown in the Eight of Chalices, with no 'graphic' connection between the meaning of the card and its image. With a few exceptions (the Sola Busca deck from the 16th century, or the Naibi by Giovanni Vacchetta, 19th century, both Italian), this form remained unchanged until the deck known as the Rider Waite Smith deck arrived around 1910. This deck presented an illustrated and highly symbolic series, even for the Minor Arcana. This theory of pictorial keys for interpreting the Tarots was such a success that today it is rare to find a deck, other than antique ones, where the Minor Arcana is not illustrated. Even though the images of the Rider Waite Smith deck were extremely evocative, they continued to present, within the image, the suits, with each specific card number. This was a specific choice. The card number is in fact very important in the Minor Arcana, and so must be immediately evident to the reader. For the Fey Tarots a different choice was made. In order not to link the images to a fixed position, cluttered with too many elements, the perception of the number of the card is entrusted to the way in which the suit is presented.

This means that the suit element increases steadily as the card number increases. The Ace of the suit is part of the Fey itself, while Number Two is poor and small and so on until Number Ten, which is the richest and most evolved.

This illustrative scheme enables certain symbols to be shown graphically which otherwise would be difficult to achieve. The Ace, of whatever suit, should represent the total potential and at the same time the total synthesis of the suit it belongs to. The representation of the Ace of Chalices as a Fey holding the chalice in her hands and becoming the chalice herself is a clear symbolic message, much more so than a hand reaching out from a cloud offering the chalice of the world (such as can be seen in traditional iconography).

Each suit has its own properties and common characteristics that identify it.

Chalices, normally associated with the element water, refer to the sphere of the sentiments and of the spirit. The Chalice is the superior nourishment that satiates the soul not the body. The water in its gushing, free flow, in its being a fountain of life and of wisdom, is the best symbol of the volatile emotional sphere.

The Chalice Fey are sweet, very intense, but never noisy or cheeky. Their eyes are deep, their thoughts comforting and there is no room for any kind of violence. In the Chalices the Fey show how to deal with the beautiful and enjoyable side of life, getting pleasure from people who are close and from little things. They show the importance of being at one with one's emotions and with what one feels at any given moment.

Pentacles, normally associated with the element earth, refer to the sphere of the world and to material possessions. Money is the element that determines every-

thing, that shows what one has, what has been built and conserved. The earth, slow, unchanging and stable, the source of each certainty and all stability, is the symbol of matter and existence in all its shapes and forms.
In the Fey Tarots the Pentacles are linked to the colours red and violet, with light touches of yellow.
The Fey that bring the Arcana of Pentacles to life are simple, not elaborate creatures; they have never deceived and have rarely been deceived. They are closely connected to objects and to places, and draw energy from their relationships with their surroundings. They demonstrate how to have without being a slave to what you possess, how to live in harmony with the material world without denying the world of magic and dreams.

Wands, normally associated with the element fire, refer to the sphere of passions and ambition - in reality to the sphere of social relationships between humans. Fire, roaring, destructive, unreliable, but also thriving, useful and hot, is the mirror of the heart of man. In fire there is a powerful carnality, a restlessness that we see reflected in our race more than in any other created thing.
In the Fey Tarot the Wands are linked to the colours green and blue, with light touches of brown.
The Wand Fey live in harmony with the trees and with nature. They act and are never still. Their essence guides them to places unknown that they have not heard of and they often make mistakes, but they are always innocent in their thirst for new emotions, energies and discoveries. They show those aspects of living that are related to doing and acting, as is usual in human society.

Swords, normally associated with the element air, refer to the intellectual sphere and to responsibility. They are a difficult, cold suit because they bear all the pain of the world: the pain and violence that we often suffer and that we inflict, at times, on our own. Perhaps it really is the role of intelligence and the intellect to question these sensations, to return them to our mind and to draw from them important lessons. The sword, Okham's razor, sharp, merciless, but also noble and sure, is like the mind of man.
Nevertheless the Sword Fey shine with great virtue. They are courageous and noble and their main objectives are the responsibility and understanding of what their actions bring; the duty not to stop at appearances and to do what is right independent of the cost and effort involved.

With Swords there is little space left for joy, but if they were free they would not need brakes. The Sword Fey are happy as such… and thanks to them all the other Fey are happy and serene, undisturbed by evil.

Each Minor Arcana is described in the following way:

The Image

In this section the card is described and an attempt is made to show the reader how to look at the card and how to link the meaning with what is illustrated.

Simple Meaning

Here a few brief key words are provided to summarise the card as much as possible. This is the departure point for the beginner and, as with the Major Arcana, it is important not to be limited just to this.

Advanced Meaning

Here the meaning of the card is described in greater detail and the reasons for the meaning are given. The simple meaning is enlarged upon and the two are joined.

The Symbols Used

The symbols present in each card are identified, giving space not just to the Arcana as a whole but to each single component.

Ace of Chalices

The Image

A child Fey, with large, gentle eyes, is immersed up to her waist in a stone container. Still, crystal water envelops her, while she raises a chalice in her hand offering water to whoever has the desire to quench their thirst. Her eyes reflect the gold of the sun, as do her nails.

Simple Meaning

Nourishment, fullness, purification, great emotions, feelings that are born and gush out.

Advanced Meaning

The first natural act that occurs when one feels an emotion is to offer. In this manner the Ace of Chalices is a gift, the feeling that surges, born from nothing and submerged by everything in its simplicity.

Often in the older Tarots, the Ace of Chalices was linked to the Holy Grail. With the Fey, the Ace of Chalices is a simple response to thirst. I am thirsty: "Well then, drink, nourish yourself, quench your thirst at the source, which is I".

Symbols Used

Few symbols were used, given the extreme synthesis of the card.

The golden eyes and nails represent a person's hidden riches.

Water is the soul's nourishment.

Two of Chalices

The Image

On a solitary rock surrounded by water two young Fey offer a chalice made from a shell and drink together. The girl is like a sophisticated mermaid, with long green hair like the sea. The boy is strong and knotty like coral.

Simple Meaning

Affinity, love, agreement, a toast, links. Promises.

Advanced Meaning

Two diverse and yet complimentary figures are joined together by a toast: a formal pact. We are in the field of feelings, with a promise of friendship, of love or even only of affinity: to connect a fragment of oneself with another person, as in a magic rite.
The chalice is designed so that two lips can drink from the same source.

Symbols Used

The sea indicates solitude and the private, intimate nature of the event.
The rocks represent removal from the sea and therefore place the accent on the exceptional nature of the event.
The two figures, male and female, indicate the growth of possible feelings. It is too soon to speak of love but there a gentle feeling stirs the heart and calms the waves.

Three of Chalices

The Image

A roughly sculpted, stone chalice abandoned on an unkempt lawn. The water from the rain is collected inside the chalice and on the rim three small Fey are playing with lots of energy. They fly and jump from edge to edge, one after the other like little hummingbirds.

Simple Meaning

To be happy in merriment, in abundance and in joy. To let oneself flow with this happy feeling.

Advanced Meaning

Happiness is one of the strongest energies that we can generate. It comes from knowing how to see the good in everything, but not only that; it also comes from knowing how to express oneself spontaneously in unexpected circumstances. Happiness is to live absolutely in the present, with no remorse for the past, nor worries for the future. Happiness, therefore, is playing and energy without reason, shape, or any other kind of prop.

Symbols Used

The unkempt garden shows how beautiful things are not always found where we expect them.

The stone chalice recalls a chess piece, like a game from a forgotten time.

The water is rainwater - pure, limpid and fresh.

The three Fey are made of energy to represent their spontaneity and their total abandon to their games.

Four of Chalices

The Image

A Fey swings lazily, suspended above a chalice full of red wine. Sleep has closed her eyes and she has abandoned herself to peace and rest. Her shadow is projected onto the wine contained in the terracotta chalice.

Simple Meaning

Boredom, resignation, waiting, lack of stimulus, satiety, sleep.

Advanced Meaning

This card demonstrates the contradictions between two aspects of man's nature. On the one hand, things have their intrinsic value and are a source of happiness. On the other hand, when there is no change things often become boring and dissatisfying. With emotions, like anything else, man looks for stimulus and not the perfect 'answer' to his needs.

Symbols Used

Wine indicates the fullness of emotions.

The suspended chair that remains immobile highlights the static nature of the stimulus offered.

The full cup indicates that we should not exaggerate with something or else we will become dissatisfied with it.

Rest is a necessary thing, which we should not have too much of however.

Five of Chalices

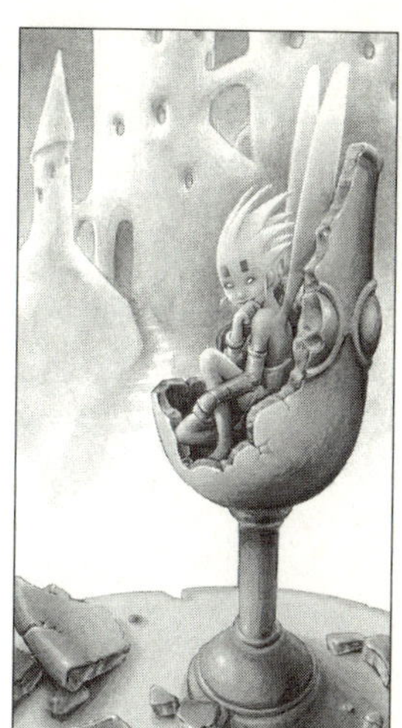

The Image

A glazed china chalice lies half-broken. In its hollow cup a small desert Fey is seated, observing the world around him, happy with his privileged position. In the background, large, imposing buildings can be seen, blurred in the distance.

Simple Meaning

Loss, joy in loss, recovering what was of value, comprehension of just proportions.

Advanced Meaning

The Five of Chalices continues the significance from the previous card. If, there, one was rich but in reality poor, here, who was poor is in fact rich. The beautiful chalice lies in pieces, but it is still beautiful and useful; it lifts up from the ground and welcomes whoever uses it. In the sentimental sphere, a happy ending is not necessarily the one we expect but can occur in a banal, more realistic way.

Symbols Used

The broken chalice is the loss the security that was depended upon.

The desert shows the apparent arid nature of the situation.

The buildings in the distance illustrate an uncertain future, still full of possibilities and discoveries.

The blue of the chalice shows that the nourishment, the water, is not necessarily outside ourselves, but exists in the value we give to things.

Six of Chalices

The Image

A small Fey with angel wings is seated on the edge of a precious chalice, which is delicately balanced on a floor of Fey eggs. The Fey is holding and playing with an egg, but is taking care not to break it.

Simple Meaning

The past, memory, turning back, a serene infancy.

Advanced Meaning

This card brings us to a confrontation with emotions suggested by memories. In traditional iconography, two children played with vases in an old villa. Here a Fey plays with an egg, in a strange world composed of the past and the future. In fact the Fey was once an egg and the egg therefore takes her back to the past, and at the same time to the Fey of the future. The chalice, like a solitary tower in this place, is the link that connects the distinct times. Like a lighthouse it guides the emotions and prevents one getting lost in nostalgia. A parenthesis from reality.

Symbols Used

The eggs are the past, infancy, origins.

They are also the future, desire, the potential that is in the process of being realised.

The game is the way whereby an argument, like time passing, can be understood and accepted.

The angel wings illustrate the Fey's total innocence.

Seven of Chalices

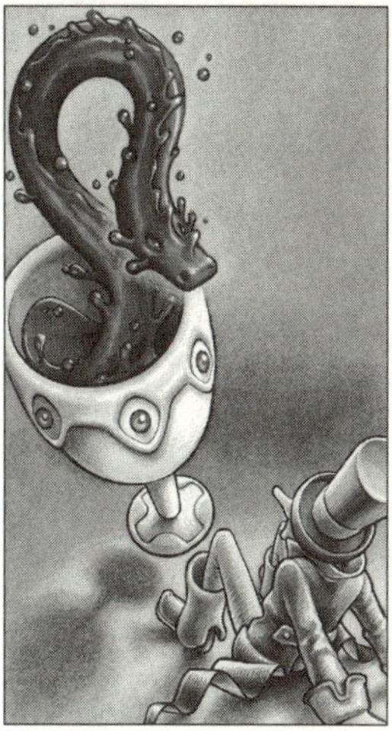

The Image

A strange Fey, dressed in an unusual manner, falls to the ground from fright, while the threatening figure of a dragon rises in the crimson wine from the silver chalice in front of him. Like a jack-in-the-box the dragon gushes upwards, but it is not ruthless, only strange and wonderful. A unreal light envelops everything.

Simple Meaning

Immediate impressions, illusions, mind games, being frightened without reason.

Advanced Meaning

The emotions consist partly of illusions and lies. Daydreams often lead to a rude awakening, yet often it is hard to distinguish them from reality. Such strongly vivid images that cannot be ignored do not allow man's spirit to control them and absorb them tranquilly, but generally affect and frighten a person tremendously. We also need to be careful when we are dealing with the emotions of others. Still waters run deep.

Symbols Used

The dragon spurting out is the symbol of all the illusions and surprises.

The unnatural light indicates that we are dealing with dramatic illusions, but not reality. Understanding needs to be regained.

The fall indicates the senses that have been momentarily lost.

Eight of Chalices

The Image

While a splendid crescent moon shines in the sky, a travelling Fey turns her back to a stairway that rises upwards through nothing until a chalice of gold and crystal is reached, full of an amber liquid.

Simple Meaning

Timidity, renouncing, moderation, respect.

Advanced Meaning

This very evocative card shows a Fey consciously renouncing her own destination, however much it appears so very near and real. Her garments show the difficulty of the journey she had to overcome, yet her shoulders are straight and strong. She renounces because she understands that she does not have the abilities; she is not the right person. This respect and this modesty with regards to something so beautiful and sacred, is the heart of emotions.

The Fey could walk up the stairs and make the chalice hers, but in taking it she might be broken and destroyed, or worse, she might break the chalice that looks so beautiful.

Symbols Used

The moon indicates the magic that governs this moment.

The stairs indicate the difficulty of the journey which is possible only to those who merit it.

Her worn and practical clothing indicate the road that the Fey has already walked.

Her posture and face indicate her determination to proceed.

Nine of Chalices

The Image

On the top of a hill an enormous chalice of heavy gold stands on green grass.

A Fey with butterfly wings, exhausted and happy, leans her back against the great chalice, while the lights of her intoxication sweeten her gentle, relaxed face.

Simple Meaning

Physical well-being, satisfaction, intoxication, fullness, and over-abundance.

Advanced Meaning

As opposed to the Four of Chalices, where fullness lead to boredom because it did not have to be worked for and was not merited, the happiness shown in this card is of a much more profound kind. It is still a happiness linked to oneself, to the fact that one has given and received with fullness and above all abandon. The well-being that is born from this sensation has no shadows, even if it disappears quickly.

Symbols Used

The beatific and sincere smile indicates the total harmony between physical and spiritual well-being.

The will-o'-the-wisp lights indicate the intoxication of joy and total satisfaction.

The relaxed position indicates peace and the desire for peace within joy.

Ten of Chalices

The Image

Once again in the midst of an immense expanse of water a chalice rises, jewelled and precious. In the chalice two Fey, a blue male and red female, sit back-to-back. Their thoughts are linked, their heads turn and they try to catch each other's eye. Nevertheless what unites them most is a rainbow of many colours released from their hands.

Simple Meaning

Joy for human beings is rarely a solitary experience. The entire sphere of emotions and affection, as can be seen in the Two of Chalices, is linked to the capacity to divide and to share the things we experience and perceive. In this card the sharing is perfect and is shown in all its glory. The old fables say that there is a pot of gold at the end of a rainbow. That gold is in the heart of he who knows how to love, he who knows how to give and how to receive.

Symbols Used

The sea indicates the vastness that retracts to leave space for joy.

The rainbow indicates the resolving of all toils and the end of the rain. It also indicates the links that unite the two hearts.

The hands from where the rainbow departs indicate that love is an offering.

Blue indicates serenity.

Red indicates passion.

Ace of Pentacles

The Image

A Fey designs a pentacle on her hand as if it is a tattoo. She is surrounded by her poor possessions in her house. Two small animals observe her. Her face is totally concentrated on what she is doing. The design on her hand is almost finished.

Simple Meaning

Links with material things. Possession of things without excess. Perfect control of the elements and of relationships. Security.

Advanced Meaning

The Fey herself becomes the pentacle via her energy and creation. In this way she creates a link that did not previously exist between the earth and the material world. This is not an cxperience without toil, but an experience that will procure for her a talisman of great power and without rival, to guide her to prosperity and to the wisdom of the earth.

Symbols Used

The painted circular symbol recalls Indian mandalas. In reality the circular symbol is one of the most ancient symbols of power in the history of humanity.

Two of Pentacles

The Image

Two Fey, both with completely different natures, meet. The first has a strong body, like a genie of the earth, seated and static. Her friendly face shows a maternal aspect and the profound wisdom of his serious gestures. Her hands, even though large, are kind, and her smile is open and sincere. The second Fey is made of energy, small, never still, continually in motion. He does some acrobatics on the stone coin that the large Fey holds in her hand, like a kind of dance that has some mysterious meaning. On the coin the head of a spade is incised.

Simple Meaning

Novelty, messages, growth, links between small and large, between material and spiritual.

Advanced Meaning

This card illustrates the link that passes between the actual immobility of the element of Pentacles and mutation and change. Pentacles are made to survive and to continue unchanged by small alterations and the vortical nature of things. As the large Fey shows, their roots are wise and deep. There is no conflict here. With regards to the other more changeable suits, Pentacles provide structure, a repetition, a point of reference.

Symbols Used

The cushion and the position of the crossed legs recall an atmosphere of fables, where every wish is possible.

The point of a spade incised on the pentacle, other than being the suit of a normal card, indicates an understanding that the dance of life is also painful.

Three of Pentacles

The Image

A Fey engraves a pentacle of painted wood with fervour and violence. On his shoulder, not heeding his rapid and improvised movements, a lizard observes his capable hand striking with the scalpel. Behind him another Fey with a covered face observes the work developing with pleasure.

Simple Meaning

Occupation, commerce, art and ability for the benefit of others. Also fervour and desire to be realised.

Advanced Meaning

In the Three of Pentacles we are confronted with the possession of objects as property and with the possession of objects as paternity. The artisan follows another's orders, but it is his heart and his able hand that generates the perfect pentacle. Things, even material things, are linked to those who create them, because it is impossible to do something without leaving a trace of our spirit behind.

Symbols Used

The lizard indicates the instinctive curiosity of man.

The covered face indicates the lack of spirit of the commissioner of the product that the artisan has carved.

Four of Pentacles

The Image

In a dark, dusty library there is a large clay pentacle, like a wheel. Books and a weak, spluttering candle stand in the background. A Fey, resigned and defeated, dressed in bright colours like a minstrel or jester, is seated on the immobile wheel. A thick chain, stronger than the Fey's puny musculature, imprisons him and chains him to the pentacle. Yet the key to the chain lies on the ground, in clear view, further away.

Simple Meaning

Avarice, jealousy, slave to riches, slave to one's habits.

Advanced Meaning

This is a sad and gloomy image, in contrast to the general gaiety of the suit. The cheerfulness that should naturally arise and fill the air with voices and song is halted: attached to a weight too heavy to be carried, it is imprisoned. One sees the imprisonment is only an illusion, because although the Fey is incapable of seeing the solution, it is there, immediate and present. All he needs is to give up the connection to what is keeping him prisoner. The real sadness is not his imprisonment but his inability to see that freedom is just a step away.

Symbols Used

The books indicate that avarice does not always refer to money, to wealth or possessions, but can concern everything.

The key and the chain indicate freedom and imprisonment.

Five of Pentacles

The Image

A simple country house where diverse Fey rest and are protected from the inclement weather outside. The pentacle that protects them is also the fire and the hearth. They in their simplicity are rich, but a shadow of monstrous appearance is approaching the large window. No-one knows if this strange figure is a threat or a small furry animal trying to find refuge and warmth.

Simple Meaning

Poverty, destitution, exclusion from what is beautiful (one's own or otherwise).

Advanced Meaning

This card has a double meaning according to whether you look from one, or the other, side of the window. The outside shows poverty and no fire or shelter; a symbol therefore of major lack. However poor one might be, though, there are people who have much less.

If seen from inside, the card is an echo of the previous card. The fear of losing what one has must not be transformed into blindness and avarice. We need to know how to accept what is foreign and diverse. We need to accept, share, and look without prejudice.

Symbols Used

The flame of the pentacle indicates heat that springs forth from the hearth of the refuge.

[This is not a proper symbol but is relevant to this section: when I had to describe to Mara how to depict the threatening shadows outside the window, I said: try to imagine Pikachu, from Pokemon, seen against the light. It is incredible where inspiration for Tarot cards might lie. Author's note.]

Six of Pentacles

The Image

A gigantic Fey, both in terms of body and statuesque face, rises above all the other Fey. A chain with a pentacle that has a star incised on it hangs around her neck is. On her two open hands, palms spread wide, small spheres of light have materialised, similar to pearls or rolls of bread. Fey of all types and ages are crowded around to take them, without daring to touch them, but rejoicing in their light, while the face of the bountiful Fey seems to indicate that there is enough of this manna for everyone.

Simple Meaning

Charity, providence, abundance, gifts, salvation.

Advanced Meaning

The significance of this card is clearly evident. To give, share, resolve the needs of others. Charity and goodwill are integral parts of sensible wealth.

A secondary significance comes from not differentiating between who will be the beneficiary. Generosity is without judgement and needs no glory.

Symbols Used

The symbol of the star on the pentacle indicates magic and providence that does not only depend on human agents.

The hairless Fey like a religious person indicates the spiritual motivations that animate goodwill.

Her nudity indicates that what is given is not only superfluous but necessary as well.

Seven of Pentacles

The Image
An elderly Fey sits comfortably napping between the roots of a knotty tree. The tree rises from the water of a lake and its leaves and flowers are made of lavish pentacles. Very relaxedly, the Fey smokes his pipe and seems content and at peace with the world.

Simple Meaning
Knowledge, peace, lack of anxiety, not obvious wealth.

Advanced Meaning
Wealth is not always ostentatious. Richness is to have no need of others, therefore, in order to be rich it is first necessary to be wise. To be able to be content and to know how to draw from what has the most in abundance. In the Seven of Pentacles richness is not in the luxuriant leaves of the tree but in the quiet of the moment. Perhaps these two things are not so far removed from one another.

Symbols Used
The pentacles, like fruit, indicate that riches arrive unexpectedly to the wise man at all times.

The water indicates the quiet and peace of emotions.

Eight of Pentacles

The Image

In an artist's grotto, a room crowded with objects and colours, the artist carefully observes a pentacle, her work of art. The painted canvas is not visible, but the care with which the young artist applies small brushstrokes and colour can be observed. Her whole body and clothes are covered in colour and paint marks.

Simple Meaning

Artisan, art, creating something that is meant to last, creative inspiration.

Advanced Meaning

The creation of things is no small matter. By application, something that did not exist before, takes shape. It could be a work of art, but also any other from of creation. The link between the material and the possibility to shape it is a very important type of intuition. Only via this perception can a creator actually generate something that is the fruit of his labours.

Symbols Used

The colours spread everywhere indicate the complexity of life and the myriad faces of things that an artist must perceive in order to infuse life into his own creations.

Nine of Pentacles

The Image

In a large opulent room a regal throne stands upon which a Fey sits, young but not beautiful. She is wearing rich garments, and a bird with multi-coloured feathers is perching delicately on her head. Her hands are composed and she is sitting formally. Behind her, there is a gathered curtain and a large chain holding up an immense gold pentacle. On the pentacle is the symbol of a bunch of grapes.

Simple Meaning

Prudence, richness, virtue linked to the administration of material things, inherited dowry, material connections between people.

Advanced Meaning

Contrary to other more personal virtues, wealth or possessions can be passed on. Therefore a person sometimes has to bear the weight of things that are not theirs or that do not derive from his own passion. This creates a link between objects and people, a link that takes place in the material world.

Symbols Used

The throne indicates the Fey's lineage and therefore signifies merits and possessions that are not the result of her actions.

The grapes indicate the possession of earthly riches, amongst the most prestigious and refined.

The bird with coloured plumage indicates the beauty and intelligence that are waiting to emerge.

Ten of Pentacles

The Image

In a room where the walls are not visible, crowded around the light of a candle, a family of Fey sits around a table. The table is the shape of a huge horizontal pentacle of heavy gold, with a similar aspect to that of a round candy. Stars hang from the ceiling, while under the table a group of small animals, also a family, are peeking out and running away.

Simple Meaning

Family, links, division of wealth, sharing of joy and abundance, celebration, feast.

Advanced Meaning

Link with the earth and with things are highlighted in the family and in the home. The table in this Arcana is nourishment itself, a source of prosperity and warmth. Symbolically it signifies the family itself and the strongest and deepest emotions. Richness, like emotions, has no meaning if kept in a safe. It must be lived. If it is not part of life and of links with others it is reduced to nothing.

Symbols Used

The circular table vaguely recalls the round table: symbol of justice and equality. Whoever sat there was on the same level as all the others.

The stars indicate how the family is a complete universe in itself.

The small animals indicate how each universe, as much as it is complete, should not isolate itself from others or behave only with concern for itself.

The candy shape of the table recalls nourishment and sweetness.

Ace of Wands

The Image

In a completely barren terrain a small green Fey is on her knees on the ground. She is the colour of emerald, or the grass in spring. On her back, instead of wings, a green bud is growing rapidly.

Simple Meaning

Creativity, birth, principle, potential

Advanced Meaning

The Ace of Wands is absolute potential, the ability to create something from nothing and to know how to create. The fire of man, energy, multiple possibilities, are all expressed in this Fey. She is conscious of what is happening and she realises that she is, in a certain sense, at the centre of a great work of magic.

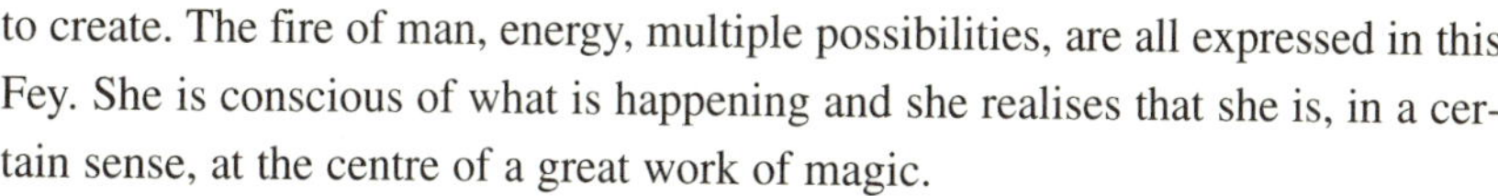

Symbols Used

The Fey, in her colour and position, resembles a frog.
The symbol signifies transformation, of oneself from roots to a tree, and then a life, which transforms the arid terrain.

Two of Wands

The Image

A fertile valley with a river flowing out of sight down below. In the sky, numerous creatures fly about, but they are too far away to see if they are other Fey or birds. On a very high tree is a nest and in the nest just one small Fey has remained. She nears the edge and prepares to jump, to learn how to fly (she has strong and beautiful wings, in fact), but she is afraid.

Simple Meaning

Fear of the unknown, the need to widen our horizons, cross a boundary.

Advanced Meaning

The world that surrounds us seems to have untouchable and unchangeable confines. We behave as if in a nest, not knowing how to fly. Everything is limited to its confines, but regardless of how large or beautiful or secure the nest is, there comes a time when we need to go further and pass the barriers that previously were unable to be crossed.

As is often the case, this is much easier to do than it seemed at first glance.

Symbols Used

Learning to fly is a symbol for all the things we do not yet know how to do.

Great height is a symbol of fear

Three of Wands

The Image

A happy and satisfied Fey observes the fruit of her labours. With a normal, not magic, spade, she has planted a strange fruit tree, the shape of a star, and this has just budded three splendid flowers that will perhaps become stars themselves. The happy, satisfied Fey sits in front of it and watches the plant grow.

Simple Meaning

Work hard in order to enjoy the fruits, initiative, ideas, doing one's part.

Advanced Meaning

Everyone needs to know how to do their part. If only one part of a job is missing, then the work cannot be completed. Once we have worked hard and done all that is necessary, we can rest and wait, observing the rewards. This moment should be relished, without being anxious about things that are already beyond our control.

Symbols Used

The star is the symbol of hope and of a beautiful and important things. The spade and the Fey's simple clothes signify that great things are possible for everyone if we want them enough.

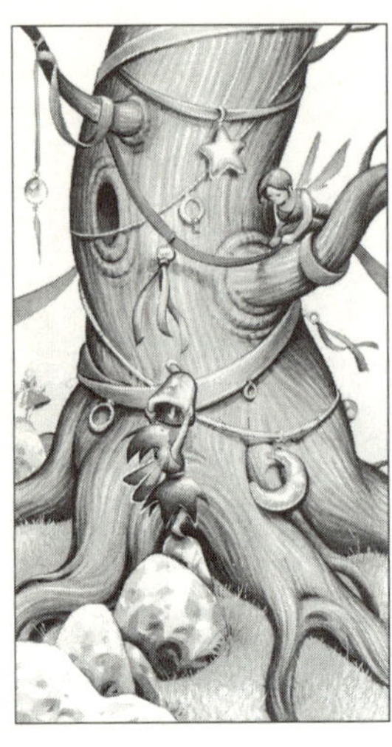

Four of Wands

The Image

Small, sweet Fey are at work on a huge tree. They are tying festoons and garlands of bells, stars and lights on to it, preparing for a feast.

Simple Meaning

Feast, celebration, agreement, tranquillity, peace, preparations of joy.

Advanced Meaning

A party does not need a reason. A party or feast happens when the heart is happy. The Fey prepare the tree for a celebration that will not only be for them. Other Fey will return from their business and find everything ready. This kind of harmonious arrangement is difficult to arrive at, but brings serenity to all the individuals who take part.

Symbols Used

The large tree is a symbol of home and stability.
The Fey are small and act with respect and humility in front of their festive task.

Five of Wands

The Image

A Fey watches a group of Fey put to the test by pulling a rope. Flying, they use the branch of a tree as a lever in this competition of strength and skill.

Simple Meaning

Struggle, training, friendly competition, physical ability, exercise.

Advanced Meaning

Even when we confront others, it is not necessary to fight nastily. To desire victory, and to do everything possible in order to obtain it, does not prevent us from being friends with our opponents and from seeing conflict as an occasion for reciprocal growth rather than a breach of trust.

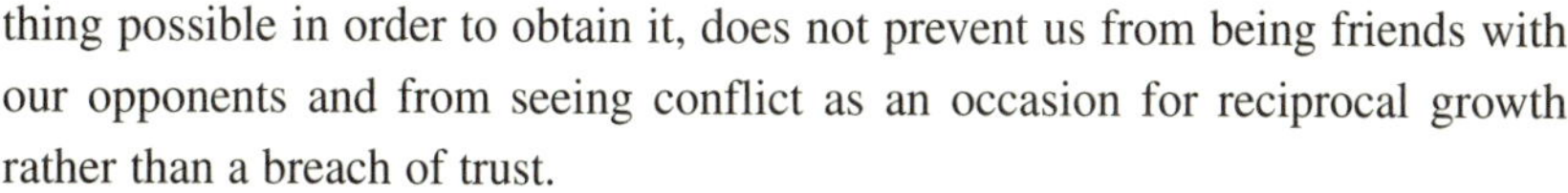

Furthermore, this card recalls the need to continually keep in shape and to never cease if we want to be ready and able when we really need to be.

Symbols Used

Here there are symbols of games and fun, inherent in the suit of wands.

Six of Wands

The Image

In the midst of a crowd of Fey in shadow, a foreign Fey moves slowly forward. He rides a large terrestrial tortoise and wears an amulet of protection around his neck. In his hand he carries a bonsai tree, an exotic species with strange leaves.

Simple Meaning

Herald, messenger, foreigner, bringer of news, honourable rival.

Advanced Meaning

A foreigner who brings a gift is not an enemy. Even if he is different and speaks another language, it is important to welcome him and try to understand him. If he turns out to be a rival, or the news he brings is not good, so be it. There is no need to be frightened beforehand. A meeting with foreigners or with someone different is always an occasion for growth and joy, and can bring with it new ideas and open new roads.

Symbols Used

The tortoise serves to indicate the distance of the journey and the slowness and seriousness that characterise it.

The bonsai tree emanates light, but its shadow is not threatening.

Seven of Wands

The Image
A small tree with luminous, precious fruit is in a corner. The spirits of evil and darkness would like to get closer to it and obscure its light, but an important Fey is standing guard and does not give an inch. In fact she beats them back with her stick.

Simple Meaning
Defence, value, protection, care, sacrifice, being on the right side.

Advanced Meaning
This card recalls the fight of good against evil and the need for courage and valour. The true enemy is often fear, because adversaries have no real substance. If this fear is defeated one can acquire the strength to resist any assault.

Symbols Used
The lights indicate something beautiful, precious and undefended
The adversaries are greater in number to highlight the value of the defender.

Eight of Wands

The Image
A Fey moves with super-human speed amongst the high branches of the trees. With small bells tied to her waist she moves, jumping and just missing the small branches.

Simple Meaning
Movement, energy, speed, motion, transformation, jumping.

Advanced Meaning
Energy is in continual movement. It does not move, it flows. All things move and change and we need to change with them, precede them, anticipate them, live with dynamism and velocity.

Symbols Used
The bells are symbols of sound. It is the only noise that you hear from this Fey. All the other symbols pertain to the idea of movement.

Nine of Wands

The Image

Two Fey are hiding in a tree cave. Both are cautious and suspicious. While one retracts into the shadow, the other, who is bigger and more self-assured, peeks out to look at the horizon.

Simple Meaning

Diffidence, vigilance, attention, never lower your guard, protection of those who are weaker.

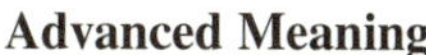

Advanced Meaning

The best way to flee from danger is to be prudent.
As usual we need to realise that we are not the only ones involved, therefore our courage needs to be mitigated by paying attention and being responsible.
At the same time this card exalts the values of perception, of attention, of the senses, of the capacity to realise things in time.

Symbols Used

The tree cave is a refuge, but it looks like a soldier's sentry box.
The Fey seem to be playing hide and seek. They are trying to hide themselves at the same time as seeking.

Ten of Wands

The Image

A little Fey is bent under the weight of a succulent fruit, much bigger than she is. Around her is an entire orchard, full of large fruit trees, but none greater than this. The Fey meanwhile looks around as if she is afraid, or as if she does not quite believe her good luck.

Simple Meaning

A heavy weight, a large prize, the fruit of one's labour, fortune.

Advanced Meaning

This card has a double meaning. On the one hand, it is a card of richness and abundance, linked to its actual value, but also to good luck. On the other hand, the weight this fortune brings cannot be denied, and the limits of strength needed to sustain it.

Perhaps this is because beautiful things cost effort.

Symbols Used

The fruit is a symbol of richness and of abundance.

The tree full of fruit is also a symbol of great abundance.

Ace of Swords

The Image

Among some rocks, a Fey clothed in red, calls a sword to her made of pure thought. It shines like fire and is the colour of blood. Its reflections reverberate on the Fey's face and on the rocks tinged with red.

Simple Meaning

Force, violence, conquest, control. Concentrate one's own thought on a particular target. Will, decision, resoluteness.

Advanced Meaning

In the Ace of Swords, the Fey calls up the sword of her own life and being, and she does this alone because she must take on this responsibility. It is a heavy burden, but it must be carried.

The Ace of Swords signifies a decision to obtain something, to do something, to get involved, to participate and accept the consequences. It means being conscious of the need to act and to deal with issues and to stop turning to others in order to resolve one's own problems.

Symbols Used

The red colour of the sword indicates the weight of this burden and the danger which is to be encountered in this moment.

The Fey's red dress indicates she has already suffered and knows what she is doing.

Her ceremonious kneeling position indicates that she understands what she is doing.

The rocks indicate solitude and therefore personal responsibility.

Two of Swords

The Image

A Fey moves decisively, brandishing two flint blades. The first blade is held in front of her eyes in order to obscure sight and to allow the spirit to observe. Conflict and latent violence can be perceived, but it is still under the control of the will. In the sky behind her is an enormous crescent moon.

Simple Meaning

A duel, a moment of truth, to deal with one's fear. The rules of conflict, the honour of war. The ability to isolate the senses and perceptions of one's own emotions and know how to regain lucidity.

Advanced Meaning

Often the Two of Swords is depicted as a blindfolded woman who offers the blades to two duellers. The concepts of justice, ordeal, ritual duel, are implicit. In normal life one rarely brandishes a sword, but equally we are often subjected to currents of violence and struggle. This card represents our ability to isolate oneself from conflicts, to remain impartial but at the same time not to be indifferent. When violence surrounds us, but is not caused by us, we need to know what is really happening and not take part; at the same time we must not ignore it or flee from it.

Symbols Used

The colour red indicates the conflict between passion and instinct and the need to be lucid.

Covering the eyes with the blade indicates a ritual gesture, a return to judging with one's inner senses.

The two blades are indications of equilibrium and our ability not to take sides.

The enormous crescent moon indicates the influence of the emotions, which put pressure on a situation.

The circle on the Fey's forehead indicates the interior vision that needs to be opened.

Three of Swords

The Image
A Fey carries the sign of the sword on his chest. Immersed in the sea, amongst the waves with the wind blowing at his back, he tries to remove the painful red mark on his chest, but it does not lose shape or consistency. The sword is part of him.

Simple Meaning
To learn pain. To suffer and not see the light nor hope. To deal with remorse, one's losses and responsibilities. Desperation, sadness, nostalgia.

Advanced Meaning
In the Christian world, evil is one of the fruits of free will, like good. Thrown out of Eden, man knows pain, suffering and obscurity. But through these trials he also discovers good and freedom. In the Three of Swords we are confronted with one's own pierced heart. The ability to perceive the difference between oneself and pain is lost, and we identify ourselves with suffering. In these moments the sea seems like a gentle caress trying to soothe the emptiness felt. We are immersed in darkness, even though dawn is breaking.
Evil cannot last forever and pain induces growth. Even if we are not able to see this and we think that the great sea is made of tears, it is nevertheless an important moment when we do not turn our back on pain but deal with it instead. This is the way to overcome it.

Symbols Used
The red sword is the symbol of blood and conflict.
The sea is the symbol of greatness, liberty and purification.
The sea is also a symbol of birth and growth, as a sea of tears can be.
The wind that blows and ruffles the Fey's wings is a sign that time has passed and that soon the pain in one's heart will be soothed.

Four of Swords

The Image
Among the ruins of an ancient palace, a Fey turns to jump, her eyes deep and shining with a cold light - the light of inevitability - while she brandishes a sword strongly. With her other hand she draws symbols in blood on her face and body. Strength, decisions, courage and also a terrible but very sweet fragility radiate from her.

Simple Meaning
To get to the bottom of things. To know how to renounce things for oneself. To lose oneself totally. To do what you must do, even though you wish it wasn't necessary.

Advanced Meaning
In traditional iconography the Four of Swords was represented by a horseman asleep on a tomb. The Fey of the Four of Swords does not sleep. She is alive, ardent, ferocious and very beautiful; but in her heart she already feels dead. She has renounced everything, and the first thing she renounced was fear. Now she prepares herself, like a knight on guard to face his destiny, whatever it is. She will not hesitate or turn back.
What makes you feel sorry for her is that she has no hope; she has abandoned her dreams; she has grown and aged too fast; she has abandoned her soul because of her 'duty'. And yet it is this decision that animates her and is the fruit of her soul and her profound sensitivity.

Symbols Used
Blood is the symbol of what the Fey no longer wishes to fear, of the pain that she will not feel, of death, of being struck and striking.
Her position is that of someone who is proud and ready to strike, even a friend, but also of resolution, generated from calmness rather than from fanaticism or anger.

Five of Swords

The Image

In an immense desert a gigantic grey sword is planted in the earth. In all this solitude a Fey calmly sits on the hilt, observing the horizon. Following the direction of her eyes, she blows on her hand and releases small sparks of light into the wind.

Simple Meaning

Reflection, mental silence, solitude, calmness and lucidity.

Advanced Meaning

Whereas the previous card of Swords demonstrated the wild, war-like side of the Fey, the Five of Swords shows its reflective side. Perhaps there had been violence in the past and perhaps there will be more in the future, but there is none in the present. The Fey reflects and observes; she isolates herself and hides from the world. And in this moment, when the silence has driven away the screams and shouts present in the preceding Arcana, new hopes and alternatives are born.

Another meaning of this card is that often conflict is not the only solution even if it seems to be, and that we should pause to reflect and find another way.

Symbols Used

The desert indicates solitude. It also indicates the lack of a road or path already trodden.

The fairy lights carried away on the wind, like seeds, indicate new hopes and opportunities.

Six of Swords

The Image

A heaving boat is anchored on a mirror of water without waves. A sword stands upright in the foreground, perhaps in the water or perhaps in the earth. A Fey with angel wings is sitting in the boat observing the sword with a dreamy air.

Simple Meaning

Journey, understanding an idea, logical passage.

Advanced Meaning

The journey that we undertake physically, in the physical world, is a mirror of the spiritual journey that we undertake. The sword in this case indicates the mind and the ability of the mind to move itself, even when the body appears to be still. Each journey brings danger, experience and discovery with it.

Symbols Used

The sword is the symbol of the mental ability to distance oneself.
The water is the symbol of a barrier or a boundary that we need to cross.
The boat is the physical means by which the mind can travel.
The Fey's expression indicates curiosity, initiative, and a desire to discover.

Seven of Swords

The Image

A Fey brandishes a sharp sword. Her body is partly flesh, partly the stones of the wall behind her, and as such a perfect camouflage. She moves her head as searching for something.

Simple Meaning

Use of any stratagem, dissimulation, or subterfuge. To know how to transform disadvantages into advantages. Act with intelligence.

Advanced Meaning

The Seven of Swords is an invitation to use prudence, and not to charge forwards with your head down. The road of principles and pride is not always the right one. At times we need to know how to hide, to conceal our intentions and abilities. Our mind is capable of inventing new ways of dealing with problems and what is obvious is not always right. When the choices seem limited perhaps there is another road, better, but hidden.

Symbols Used

The chameleon-like capacity of the Fey is an invitation to adapt to what surrounds us, without losing oneself.

Eight of Swords

The Image
An apparently undefended Fey is a prisoner in an empty, oval room. A precious sword, decorated with arabesques, is fixed in the ground a little distance from her. Red bands bind her legs, arms and wings.

Simple Meaning
Imprisonment, to be impotent and defenceless. The ability to support arrogance, insolence, the use of force against one's rights. The refusal to bend in the face of adversity and to stoop to compromise.

Advanced Meaning
The Fey prisoner appears weak, defeated, at the mercy of whatever force brought her to this situation. Yet she has not lost her spirit and does not accept that she must bow to the stronger. The sword that hangs over her is both a threat and a promise of freedom, as it could serve the prisoner as well as the jailer. When we are under pressure, under attack, or victim of an injustice, we should not cry and wait to be saved, but react instead, be strong and never renounce our own identity.

Symbols Used
The imprisoned wings indicate an attempt to negate the Fey's actual nature. The sword indicates that a resolution is near at hand, for better or worse.

Nine of Swords

The Image

A Fey is bent over, turned into herself, overwhelmed by her bitter pain. Above her hangs a sword of cold steel, held only by a thread. The tip is aimed at her unprotected back. The Fey's body is red and her face is covered by her hair. In the distance, though, a limpid night sky and stars shining brightly illuminate a stairway that leads out of this deep abyss.

Simple Meaning

Remorse, pain, self-destructive will, surrender, abandonment, nightmare, desperation, deep suffering.

Advanced Meaning

Again Swords are given the unpleasant task of handling and describing the human soul's relationship with pain. Pain hurts but it is part of life and we must not flee it, ignore it, or negate it. When it comes, pain is real and true, and the tarots must accept this. This card deals with remorse, responsibility, and loss. It describes the moment when not only is there no more hope, we do not even want to hope. We wait only for the pain to stop, in the worst and most terrible way.
Hope, however, does not just depend on us. It is there even if we cannot see it, and pain is not able to shut every door and cloud every light. Not even the pain that comes from within and seems to swallow everything.

Symbols Used

The hanging sword is like the sword of Damocles that could strike at any moment and bring ruin.
The stairs are the symbol of the exit from below ground and a return to light.
Leaden grey is the colour of desperation that engulfs all details.
The stars are the lights that shine. They are like tears, because at times, tears help.

Ten of Swords

The Images

In front of a mysterious symbol, a Fey disintegrates and changes into sand. Her sword breaks and shatters, and everything crumbles.

Simple Meaning

Breaking up, destruction, annihilation, end. To succumb, final strike.

Advanced Meaning

This card seems to bring only negative symbols and inauspicious omens with it. Nevertheless, it is exactly in such moments that it is necessary to look carefully for the hidden meanings and nuances in meaning. It is not always possible to win. At times we lose and are defeated, but this is only a new beginning. A Fey can never die, unless she wishes to do so. She is transformed and her essence remains in other things. This card also indicates the end of conflict and of the destruction of those who do not know how to stop. The seal on the wall is truth and the end that destroys anger and dark passions.

Symbols Used

The sand is the symbol of time. It indicates that all things have an end, ours and those of others, whether powerful or weak.

The sword that breaks is the conclusion of the battle and the end of pain.

Red indicates the threat one feels, and also indicates that it went too far.

The seal is truth, the external intervention that completes everything.

THE COURT CARDS

The name “Court Cards” generically indicates a subset of the Minor Arcana, in particular the King, Queen, Knight and Knave. These cards are historically different from the rest of the numerical cards as they are illustrated cards that have been in existence since the earliest Renaissance Tarots. When Tarots began to be used for cartomancy (which occurred three centuries after they had been created), the first esoterics paid attention to this difference in design and attributed a very particular role to the 'court cards': they were to represent specific individuals, not just situations, but archetypes and physical people.
Over time this clear division changed and the idea of 'fortune-telling', which once characterised it, faded. Nevertheless, these four cards for each suit have always had a specific nature.

This section introduces and describes the court cards.

Personality
The physical character of the person is described.

Image
The image of the court figure is described.

Simple Meaning
The key words pertaining to the meaning of the card are provided.

Advanced Meaning
The significance of the Arcana is expanded upon.

Knave of Chalices

Personality
In youth it is not always possible to distinguish between the emotions that will last and those that will vanish in the morning.

Image
A young noble knave, in Balinese dress and hair-style, looks into a chalice with a questioning air. From the chalice a dream-fish emerges and looks at him.

Simple Meaning
Adolescence, studious youth, a curious person, contemplative spirit.

Advanced Meaning
The fish that emerges from the chalice is an ancient symbol that indicates the materialization of the mind's imaginings. Therefore, the unexpressed question that the knave asks the chalice of water is actually a question to himself. In the Knave of Chalices we are faced with hunger for emotions and sentiments and inexperience in dealing with them.

Knight of Chalices

Personality

Violence also exists in the emotions... just as overwhelming sentiments or emotional blackmail exist. The Knight of Chalices has realised this and it disturbs him, because it clashes with the idealised image he is used to. Nevertheless, he has not yet decided whether to accept this challenge or to stop believing in the innocence of love.

Image

A knight emerges from the sea riding a giant lobster. He manoeuvres a sword and a chalice in his hands, weighing one against the other.

Simple Meaning

Dreamer, seducer, suitor, poetic soul.

Advanced Meaning

The Fey knight who rises from the sea finds himself on the boundaries of pure sentiment and his strong natural aggression. For this reason he debates between the chalice and the sword. He can choose whether to deceive and receive love without giving it in exchange, playing a game with emotions without participating, or else he can choose to risk and become involved, renouncing his strength and all his advantages.

Queen of Chalices

Personality

The Fey Queen of Chalices is capable of listening. Her strengths are empathy and understanding. Even in the depths of the sea, from where she rises, she is perennially disposed towards others, in generosity and friendship.

Image

Sitting amongst many cushions, in an Oriental way, the Queen of Chalices agitates a large and bulky chalice full of water. She is not thinking of herself, but her acute senses and reflexes enable her to hear everything that is going on around her.

Simple Meaning

Comprehension, listening, empathy, attention, delicate soul.

Advanced Meaning

Comprehension and listening are the keys to this Arcana. The Queen does not limit herself to perception only, but also empathises. Her words soothe pain and it is removed, even though it is not in her power to heal.

King of Chalices

Personality

The King of Chalices is the perfect master of his emotions. He does not bury them nor tame them, but is able to live with them perfectly. He, like the Knave, interrogates a chalice, but this time he looks to the chalice for the answers that he does not know and that come from reality.

Image

One of the most noble Fey, whose only crown is a band of gold, he holds a chalice of precious metal, moulded in the shape of the world. He is smiling, but his gaze remains fixed and intense.

Simple Meaning

Experience, impartiality, emotional distance, whimsical soul.

Advanced Meaning

With maturity, emotions do not vanish but become more removed and deeper. Just as waves in the sea are more difficult to see when the sea is deep, so are the great emotions of the king. They run deep but envelope every fibre in his body.

Knave of Pentacles

Personality
Inexperience, even in the material field, brings about a desire to explore and to experiment. Without fear, he tries to widen the spaces he is used to and to perceive more of the world.

Image
A young Fey, with no sign of preoccupation on his face, flies on a swinging pentacle, engraved everywhere. The signs of the moon and the stars can be seen and perhaps, on the side where he sits, the sign of the sun can be seen too.

Simple Meaning
Application, study, knowledge, enquiring spirit.

Advanced Meaning
This card indicates exploration of spaces and places, rather than introspection or soul-searching. Restlessness is characteristic of youth and also of the suit of Pentacles, and is transmitted by this errant motion and in this continual quest for answers about one thing and another.

Knight of Pentacles

Personality
This Fey is linked to the earth and to his personal belongings, but his duty and service towards others have led him far from them. This upsets him, but this distance helps him understand the real importance of the things he loves.

Image
On an unknown road, this Fey rides a rabbit. A pentacle hangs from the bit and a castle stands in the background on the right, which the Knight's gaze lingers on.

Simple Meaning
Responsibility, honesty, service, loyal spirit.

Advanced Meaning
Loyalty is not aimed at only one person or at duty in a strict sense, to words said or to promises. Loyalty is a sentiment that is linked to coherence in things we belong to and love. Through loyalty, with regards to our values or our origins, it is possible to discover a part of our actual identity.

Queen of Pentacles

Personality

Gaiety, without pretext or hidden ends, is painted on the face of this young girl. She seeks company and human contact, and is willing to give the same in exchange. She is ready to give and also ready to assert herself, without being able to pause and reflect on relationships.

Image

A young girl, with a spontaneous and delicate air, plays with a pentacle that is divided into two halves: one the sun, the other the moon. Her hands rest on the pentacle as if it were a musical instrument, and a smile plays on her lips.

Simple Meaning

Opulence, magnificence, flirtatiousness, aesthetic spirit.

Advanced Meaning

In the suit of Pentacles, the Queen is a little rebellious. Her ability to disregard things is not in harmony with the rest of the suit, but it is precisely for this reason that she manages to communicate and deal with others well. Her roots are strong like the earth, but her look and her thoughts are light, never tired from troubles.

King of Pentacles

Personality

Continual worrying about success and achieving results has made the King of Pentacles very powerful, but older than his time. Now he has many regrets, but just as much joy.

Image

A city of great riches, where a powerful disc stands out, the symbol of the pentacle: the King is in the foreground, with no crown, a hard and decisive face, hair the colour of fire and a veil of sadness shadowing his expression.

Simple Meaning

Value, ability in business, success, practical spirit.

Advanced Meaning

The prosperity of all those who depend on him. As can be seen from his clothes, not at all luxurious or magnificent, this Fey with no crown does not need effigies of power to be powerful. He has dedicated his life to success and to security and has now obtained this, not only for himself but for all those who look to him.

Knave of Wands

Personality

The quest for the right words and deeds to do is a complicated task. Action has given way to the imagination, but only for a short spell. This Fey is in love with life, but has not yet decided what to do.

Image

A young Fey, with a blue unicorn horn, dreamily observes an egg, which is suspended a few centimetres above her hand. From the egg a luminous bud grows. On the table in front of the Fey, a leaf of white, rolled parchment can be seen, together with a goose feather and an inkpot.

Simple Meaning

In love, creative, sentimental spirit.

Advanced Meaning

The egg with the twig that is evoked from the power of the Fey, is the symbol of the passion that is within her heart. This passion is not sterile or abandoned, but is a passion that must bear fruit, as soon as the young Fey is able to find a way to express her real feelings. This is not necessarily to be interpreted as love for another person. Love has many forms, and sensual love is just the most simple, but certainly not the only one.

Knight of Wands

Personality

There are no limits or boundaries for this Fey. Her travels depend only on her will and curiosity, on hers thirst for new experiences. Each thing, colour, sound, or smell, bring smiles and joy. The Knight of Wands throws herself enthusiastically into whatever she undertakes.

Image

Among the highest trees, far from earth and almost in the kingdom of the heavens, a laughing, confident Fey rides a multi-coloured bird, standing in her stirrups to push her mount even higher.

Simple Meaning

Traveller, adventurer, player, enthusiastic spirit.

Advanced Meaning

To live life as an adventure means dealing with every obstacle and barrier as a challenge. In this way the more difficult things appear to be, the stronger the stimulus to deal with them. It is also a violent force, but not hostile and destructive, only at times a little egocentric.

Queen of Wands

Personality

This Fey was once a rebel, a hooligan, a difficult character. All the corners and edges of her heart have been burnt out of the life that she feels within. Now she feels only the wonderful sensation of creation and of being creative.

Image

A beautiful Fey with long green hair tied behind her, reaching down to her waist. With her body tattooed with leaves and fronds, she turns and smiles. A hand skims over the crown she has on her head, while the other hand is placed over her pregnant stomach.

Simple Meaning

Creator, cultivator, healer, generative spirit.

Advanced Meaning

This card shows how pain or restlessness can disappear by themselves, cancelled by the need for something greater. The primary instinct, that of creation, not only of another life but of anything at all, is at the heart of the happiness of this card. Another meaning of this card is an invitation to deal with difficult people and situations gently, because this gentleness will sooner or later find an echo in the other's character or the event.

King of Wands

Personality

The King of Wands has no age. Like all the Fey his appearance is more congenial to his character and not vice-versa. He has therefore decided to remain a child and to see everything as if for the first time. This does not make him inexpert, however, but wise and knowing.

Image

Sitting on some cushions on the branches of a tree is a child king. The candles around him have made him another crown. Between his hands he holds a perfectly spherical crystal ball and his wise gaze looks ahead.

Simple Meaning

Reflection, wisdom, farsightedness, concentrated spirit.

Advanced Meaning

To perceive things each time, to dedicate attention to everything, even when it seems banal and discounted, to ask practical, not intellectual questions about what or why something is happening, these are the keys to remaining youthful: rich in strength, energy and stimulation. Thanks to this way of seeing things it is possible to concentrate oneself, focus and therefore obtain the things that otherwise would seem way beyond our limits.

Knave of Swords

Personality

This Fey does not love war and battle, even though he is skilful in both. His nature is divided into two parts: one that desires peace and one that pushes him to excel at war. For this reason he never strikes first but always last.

Image

A Fey made from two contrasting halves. One is the colour of violet and the other blue. His arms move about in martial positions and play with a broadsword that remains brandished, yet not held. Jewellery the shape of rings and circles completes the image.

Simple Meaning

Vigilance, attention, guard, defensive spirit

Advanced Meaning

Knowing one's strength can bring a person to use it, when they should withhold instead. Above all, when the conflicting situation is not clear and there are doubts in one's soul, one should be able to measure one's response, know how to be patient, and know how to defend oneself without being aggressive.

Knight of Swords

Personality

Passion and fire have the better of this Fey. She has thrown herself into the battle without any regard for her own safety. She does not fight with anger, but for good reasons. However, her anger and adrenalin have made her lose sight of the reasons. In this case it is not she who brandishes a weapon, but she herself is a weapon in the hands of her passions.

Image

A white dragon with great scales against a background of fire or blood. It is ridden by a Fey with blood-injected eyes and her sword unsheathed, who shouts out a challenge.

Simple Meaning

Ability, courage, impulsiveness, anger, fighting spirit.

Advanced Meaning

The loss of control in oneself, abandoning oneself to fury, momentarily cancelling reason: these things happen. Nevertheless often the pain that we do not feel in that moment from the wounds inflicted and received, hurt a hundred times more later on when we have time to think over all that occurred.

Queen of Swords

Personality

This Fey has much sorrow and perhaps much remorse as well. However she has grown and become wise. She does not cry because the time for crying is still far away. Only when everything is put right and she has done all that is possible to remedy pain, will she then dedicate some time to herself. For now she has sworn to herself that she will never make a mistake again and that she will always chose the difficult road, if that is the right road.

Image

In a grey, though not gloomy or squalid, city, the Queen of Swords is clothed in fur. She is not wearing a crown nor a sword, because both these things have become part of her, engraved on her forehead with a ruby. Her lips are blue, like someone who has no heat within them, yet she is beautiful; beautiful and untouchable like ice.

Simple Meaning

Sadness, responsibility, loss, courageous spirit.

Advanced Meaning

True courage comes from knowing how to react to a situation. Whatever has happened, whatever has passed, the blame, the pain, we are always faced with a new beginning. It may be difficult and painful, but it offers hope, and uses the strength that has matured. Courage means not repeating previous errors: it means to grow and not give up.

King of Swords

Personality
The King of Swords possesses the burden of command and decision making. He has found himself faced with the responsibility of making difficult and hard decisions and to decide the fate of others. For this reason he finds it hard to be happy. However, he has never stopped feeling emotions, nor wishing that every war would end, so that the Fey too can rest and put down their arms.

Image
The King of Swords sits on a sober throne carved of cold stone, his body tense and restless, his red hair blowing in the wind, dressed in armour. His face and neck have wounds that have never healed, marking his metal-coloured skin with red lines. A whirling wind surrounds him, blowing the autumn leaves with it, but his expression is neither angry nor proud. He has kind eyes in that severe looking body.

Simple Meaning
Strength, decision, power, authoritative spirit.

Advanced Meaning
The possibility of choice brings with it great responsibility. We need to bear in mind the consequences of all actions and realise that these affect others, not just ourselves. Others that we do not know, who are far away, but often others whom we love or who are connected to us. This is a heavy burden as there is never a perfect, or right, choice, but only the choice that we make, full of all its consequences.
A perfect choice does not exist, but we must choose nonetheless.

DIVINATORY SPREADS

What are divinatory spreads?

Many people will already have heard these words so please excuse any repetitions for the benefit of the 'not yet expert' Tarot readers.
Knowing the meaning of the cards is not enough to create the number of possibilities and multiplicity of this art. In fact the significance of a card depends on the position in which it is found.
By placing the cards face down in a particular spread, and linking each position to a question, the Tarots provide the answers to many questions.
For example, the card Strength, (whose meaning is strength) in the position that indicates “what we have need of”, simply means that there is a need for strength or force. A more complicated situation arises when the same card appears in the position that indicates, for example, “obstacles”. In this instance it can be interpreted as a fear of using force and an inability to improve what we are doing.

The following section provides some instructions that can be useful for obtaining different results and also for beginning to understand the Tarots used in this particular deck.

Rituals

One important, though not essential, thing I suggest you do is to create a small ritual to follow each time the Tarots are used. It might be the way the cards are shuffled, or how one sits, or any other small gesture to which we attribute a meaning.
Personally, I do not believe that these rituals have any intrinsic 'power', but I do know that these gestures help to focus one's concentration. Reading the cards is a meditative experience, and an interior silence is necessary to achieve this. A ritual not only helps the reader to create a situation of serenity within himself, it also helps the person to whom the cards are being read overcome any nervousness, scepticism or chaotic thought.
Examples of rituals are not to sit with crossed legs; not to wear metallic objects; to shuffle the cards, or have them shuffled, a certain number of times or in a certain way; to light a candle; to close one’s eyes and remain in silence for a few

seconds.

It is important that these gestures are given a certain significance, so that they are actually linked to what is happening. For example, if one decides to shuffle the cards three times, the first time might represent the past, the second the present and the third the future. The gestures are not important in themselves; they are important for emphasising the procedure and the spirit that accompany them.

Dream, Joy, Magic

This simple spread of three cards is for using for oneself rather than for other people. The aim is not to interrogate past, present or future, but rather to help focus the positive energies a reader needs in order to read the cards for others.

Once the cards have been shuffled, three cards are chosen, as in the illustration. The cards have the following meanings:

1. The Dream
This card shows all the energies that are the limit of what we are capable of perceiving. It shows what could happen, all the possibilities and opportunities. It shows our ability to withdraw from the real, oppressive and limited, world for a moment and learn wisdom and understanding on this journey.

2. Joy
This card shows a reason for being joyful and happy. Remove all other influences and concentrate on the present moment of happiness. The reason for joy emerges from obscurity, drowning the heart and eyes with laughter.

3. Magic
This card indicates the World of the Fey, which we need to come into contact with in order to use this deck properly. Who are the Fey? They are 'being' as opposed to 'having'; now as opposed to then; the possible as opposed to the limits. The magic is the card that indicates what can and will be if one believes strongly enough. It indicates the possibility of what might happen.

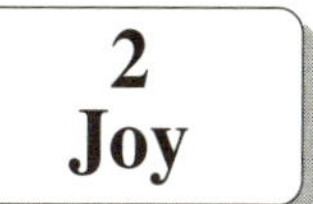

The Fey Child

This spread is in fact a useful exercise for reflecting on the cards and for meditating. It is actually very simple, even if it seems complex to beginners.

Two cards are taken and placed face to face, as shown.

1. The Mother
This card represents the female generative principle.

2. The Father
This card represents the male generative principle.

It is clear at this point that the Fey represented are metaphors for existential universal concepts. Try to imagine, while meditating on this, that the two concepts, united, generate another and move in a joint direction. They add to each other, but the result is more than the sum of what they originally were.
Imagine how the child Fey will be, what concept it brings, what form it will take. As mentioned above, this is a meditative exercise and does not bring any answers, only the wisdom that can be gained from this experience.

1 2

The Cross of the Four Kingdoms

This spread is useful for analysing a situation or a particular state of mind. The cross of the four kingdoms is an ideal point in the world of the Fey, where the four suits - Chalices, Pentacles, Wands and Swords - are at an equal distance. In whatever case, person or situation, the four components of the Tarot are present, even though not with the same influence.

The cards are divided into 5 piles: one for each suit and one for the Major Arcana. One card from each of the minor suits is then taken and placed as illustrated.

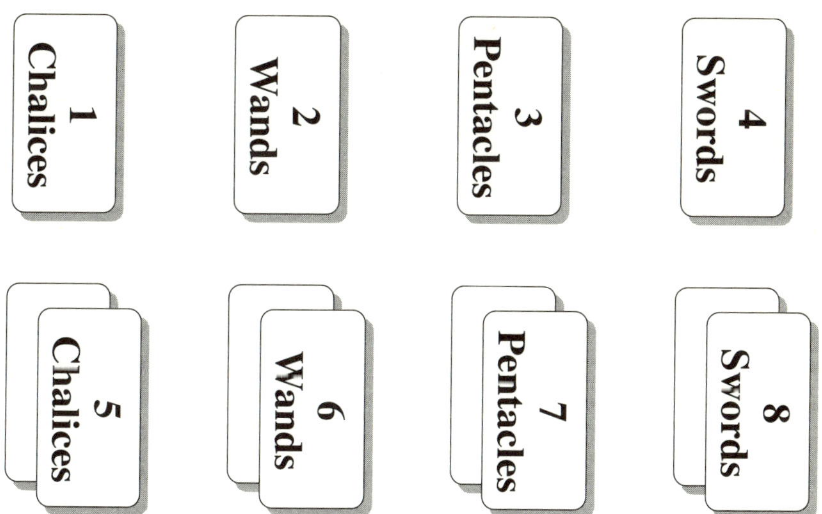

1. Chalices
This card indicates the emotive component of the situation and the sentimental aspect that animates it.

2. Wands
This card indicates the conflicting actions and the desires in the situation.

3. Pentacles
This card represents the pragmatic and material component, tied to the facts of the situation.

4. Swords

This card indicates the rational part and the suffering that is inherent in every situation.

Once the cards have been read in this way, shuffle all the remaining cards, and place them on top of the four cards already chosen. This time, unlike before, there will not necessarily be a card of the corresponding suit in each position.
Repeat the reading adding the meaning of the new card to the pre-existing one.

The Six Stars

This divinatory spread is more general in design and allows many questions to be posed and therefore a possible solution.

Place the cards in the following manner:

1. The Morning Star

This card gathers the morning energies, those of re-awakening and of birth.
The Tarot that occupies this position indicates the way the querent initiates things and how they were placed in the past, with respect to the actual situation.

2. The Midday Star

This star gathers the energies of maximum expansion, of consequent results and of maximum energies.
This Tarot therefore indicates the present and the way in which a situation has reached its peak.

3. The Evening Star

This card gathers the energies of conclusions and of decline. Here things stop and are remembered, when they are no longer shining.

This card represents the future, but not the future that will be, but rather the future that would be if the querent takes no action to change it.

4. The Star of Dreams

This card gathers all the magic energies that govern the situation. Here we are dealing with what cannot be described or rationalised.

This Tarot indicates the unexpected influences that can modify a situation, even if they are not understood. Certainly they are not foreseen and modify what was written on the Evening Star.

5. The Star that is not a Star

This card gathers the fears, perplexities, indecisions and obstacles that are interposed between the querent and the situation.

It identifies the forces opposing the querent, which have to be neutralised.

6. The Star that reflects every light

This card represents the actions of the querent, and is in direct opposition to the preceding card. The querent's actions should not be hindered by obstacles and fears and they influence the evening star and the star of dreams.

The Fey Tarot is an enchanting deck: full
of life and energy.
Just like fairies, it contains no shadows
– or only those that we ourselves bring –
and no evil, violence or maliciousness.

The cards are interwoven with Dreams
that soar above daily routine;
with Joy that allows us to come through storms
and tempests without losing our way;
and with Magic, the vital breath of every Fey.

The heart of the Fey is linked to that of a child. It is as sweet and delicate as the dew, as well as simple and kind – yet it is also ancient, noble and courageous: in tune with the magic of the entire world.